OUR OWN FELICITY:

We Make Or Find

C.L. Corey

Plymouth, Michigan
November, 2001

Copyright © 2004 by C. L. Corey

All rights reserved. No part of this book shall be reproduced or transmitted in any form or by any means, electronic, mechanical, magnetic, photographic including photocopying, recording or by any information storage and retrieval system, without prior written permission of the publisher. No patent liability is assumed with respect to the use of the information contained herein. Although every precaution has been taken in the preparation of this book, the publisher and author assume no responsibility for errors or omissions. Neither is any liability assumed for damages resulting from the use of the information contained herein.

ISBN 0-7414-2216-6

Published by:

INFINITY
PUBLISHING.COM

1094 New DeHaven Street, Suite 100
West Conshohocken, PA 19428-2713
Info@buybooksontheweb.com
www.buybooksontheweb.com
Toll-free (877) BUY BOOK
Local Phone (610) 941-9999
Fax (610) 941-9959

Printed in the United States of America

Printed on Recycled Paper

Published November 2004

DEDICATION

To all the young people everywhere

What we have loved,
Others will love,
and we will teach them how.

Prelude: Wordsworth

NOTE ON THE AUTHOR

Not yet six years of age, I walked four miles by the section lines across the Montana prairies to a one-room schoolhouse; to the side was a teacherage and in back a boys on the right, girls left, with a barn in between for horses. No Headstart, no remedial; one $80 a-month teacher and about 30 students, who learned to read, write, do arithmetic, and learned history. In high school we were told in 1939 that we would have to go to war to end the idea that the State should tell people how to think and live. When war came a million of us volunteered; I served a full tour as combat pilot over Europe. Home, I became a Harry Truman liberal, and received a Ph.D. in Engineering from The University of Michigan in 1951.

Saw my party devastated by "peace demonstrators" in 1968, and some thousand more of them urged "kill your parents", "bring down the system", burn the campus, at Kent State. The Vietnam War was started by the "intellectual's" "best and brightest", who destroyed the Viet government then demanded "withdrawal", and blamed America for a criminal war. An unpopular President was given a nearly unprecedented reelection majority, for essentially ending America's active part in the war, making peace with China, and obtaining a peace treaty with Hanoi, the negotiators for which received Nobel Peace Prizes. He was then denounced, driven from office, and the peace treaty abandoned for a Communist victory.

That all of this, from Franklin Roosevelt's "day in infamy" on, was based on lies, open, bare-faced lies, began to dawn upon me in 1968.

I started a search for why and how the war to end evil Statism had resulted in not only the spreading of it around the world, especially in America, but also in starting a war on humanness and civilization. After twenty years, I felt I understood generally what had happened, and began to write it down. *Our Own Felicity* is an attempt to generate a desire, a will, and a way, to regain humanness as central to all that makes life worthwhile. It will be produced and distributed with the help of the Committee for Correspondence, an intended nonprofit organization, to all who will become a part of the greatest and most essential movement in a millennium.

www.committeeforcorrespondence.net

Join with people in discussions directed at an understanding of, and organizing for moving to rebuild, our human society. The Committee asks not for your money but for your participation in a momentous adventure.

Manuscript and text prepared by:
THE LETTER WRITER
Plymouth, MI

CONTENTS

CHAPTER	TITLE	PAGE
	PREFACE	i
PART ONE		
I	INTRODUCTION	1
I	THE WAR	7
III	THE DEMONIC DREAM	12
IV	THE SUPREME QUESTION	17
V	SIMPLE HUMANNESS	30
PART TWO	INTRODUCTION	44
VI	WORLD WAR II	46
VII	WAR ON HUMAN SOCIETY	63
VIII	CONSPIRACY	79
IX	HATRED AND TRUTH	112
X	ON GUIDANCE	162
NOTES	ON ARYANS	27
	ON WWII	61
	CONSPIRACY REORGANIZED	94
	ON RACISM	136
	ON THE JEWISH QUESTION	154
	ON RELIGION	166
	REFERENCES	171
	INDEX	191

PREFACE

"The consequence of the abdication of authorities which had stood, however imperfectly, for a common social purpose, was the gradual disappearance . . . of the very idea of purpose," wrote R.H. Tawney early in the past century. A half century earlier J.S. Mill had implied the Western purpose in his definition for "culture", as "the knowledge which one generation gives to its successors for at least *keeping up if not raising*" in humanness. What could be more positive, more supremely important, next to survival itself? Yet the perception was forced in the Sixties that culture was merely behavior, neither good nor bad, and certainly devoid of purpose; mere entertainment as sports, the infantile, and erotic. Earlier Tocqueville had warned that if the people allowed motivation for self government to fade and the State to usurp all initiatory purposes, they would "gradually fall below the level of humanness".

It is very myopic and a misjudgment of the depth of the disaster into which Western civilization has been sliding for centuries to claim that it happened in the Sixties, or even in the past century. The slide began almost five centuries ago when Machiavelli recognized that adherence to the Christian purpose was slipping and sensed the opportunity for intellectuals to make promises and take over. He likely was aware that the ancient god-king tyrannies were ruled by intellectual bureaucracies, and he probably had their exalted positions in mind, not the modern totalitarianism which grew from his idea. It takes directed effort, motivation, responsibility, and acceptance of impositions of many kinds, and perseverance to maintain a human society, as to build a family, a company, or to become an athlete or musician.

A major purpose of this book is to bring truth about our past and present, and to arouse hope, with motivation and conviction, that a productive and organized recovery of a human society is not only credible but that success is straightforwardly achievable. The intent is to induce people to believe, and to comprehend, that this is their opportunity to participate in the most human and noble effort, to save and to rebuild our self governing human society. Our regime's manipulation of public perceptions, both before and after 9-11, makes organizing for that effort imperative, and the help of all is needed.

And immediately! At the last minute, in *Atlantic Monthly* (Mar. 02), came the following: "Bewildered, depraved children . . . downright menace of children . . . anxiety and frustration", without purpose, irrational. Then "Gangs . . . Los Solidos, LaFamilia, Latin Kings . . . from played out industrial cities . . . sensed a virgin market . . . town kids joined the crime lords . . . in drugs, heroin . . . learned extortion in schools, drug routes . . . girls providing lodging, credit cards, sex . . . state's jails . . . gang recruiting centers". To "Our kids, the MTV generation . . . these guys look like TV stars . . . they join up!" "Adults not bothering to reach out." Since "World War II adolescents chafing against an unheeding social system . . . why . . . children plotting to blow up their worlds . . . goal to mesmerize the middle class with violence . . . a purifying attempt to intervene against nothingness".

"The state's growing arrogation of power . . . expresses both fear and contempt for children". But the marketplace "has spent hundreds of millions of dollars exploiting their emotions and thought processes . . . (B)ehavioral sciences advise companies on the latest semiotics of 'cool' . . . what teens think . . . want . . . aspire to be . . . Translates in the marketplace as hypersexuality, addiction . . . seedbed of apocalyptic nihilism." (The killers of the Dartmouth faculty couple, Jan. 2001, "two bright kids" and "well-liked" not misfits, Robert Tulloch and James Parker, "were bored with their lives.") And who gets blamed? Why those old scarecrows: capitalism, guns, skin heads. The real enemies are in Hollywood and New York, the crooks and renegades in the White House, in Congress, the bureaucrats, public education, even in churches, as will be documented.

There are many developments in the modern world

which, though detrimental or destructive of human society, people generally would be reluctant to forgo. Most notable of these is mass production which degrades the individual and corrupts society. Others are urbanization, mass culture, and even agriculture which made serfs of noble hunters. But the inhumanness and loss of survival as a fixed purpose due to agriculture, have largely been offset and accommodated.

Not only has there been no significant effort to correct for the others: mass production, urbanization, and mass culture; they have in ways been promoted as subversive to human society, for the advent of Statism. Intellectuals are no more apt to search for means to palliate these problems than are educationalists to restore education, jurists to reaffirm a Constitution of meaning, or the mainstream to cease undermining essential social institutions.

C.L. Corey

PART ONE   INTRODUCTION

Imagine the soul shrivelling agony, the despair, pain, hate, and abandonment of life itself, that must have long festered in the minds of the young school-killers, in a number of states. Worse yet, how many more exist today in this torment, but for a thousand reasons have stopped short of the brink. Surely only the tip of a widespread pathology has been seen.

"Oh, God! I'm so close to killing people. So close, I'm evil and want to kill and give pain. I hate myself for what I have become." So wrote a 15 year-old Oregon boy a few days before killing his parents, his older sister, and shooting up his school, wounding 25 others, then looking into death himself.

His parents were both teachers, his older sister a gifted student and an athlete, the pride of their father. Kip had developed a "learning disability", lacked physical grace, characteristics recently documented for "fatherless" boys. A deepening rift with his father, preoccupation with heavy-metal, guns, rejection by a girl he liked, then taking a gun to school and being expelled "apparently triggered the rage", but no visible parental concern. He was left at home, shorn from human attachments, staring at a black hole.

The Colorado killers, in their own high school, received bizarre hands-on instruction in killing, death, suicide. One class assignment produced videos that glorified bloody violence. Much has been made of their "trenchcoat" alienation, with gross misunderstanding. Alienation like homosexuality in youths has often been pushed on them. No one wants them; pretending to is only a defense. And in school this was supported by "Values Clarification"; "make your own values", thus denying the central purpose of culture and education. Harris, the leader in Colorado, recognized his danger, as did Kip in Oregon, and tried to escape to the Marines. That door was slammed shut five days before the blow-up by the hyperactivity drugs he had been fed.

Humanness and the maintenance of a human society must be taught; it requires work, conviction, responsibility, perseverance, and impositions as do all purposes, as becoming an athlete or musician. Instead of admitting the appalling reality of the social corruption and dysfunction and moving to provide a more human society and education, the renegade bureaucracies, both public and private, have used these horrible incidents to beat the drums for more empowerment of the State: more gun control, police, shrinks, metal detectors, walls. "Never before has a generation of teenagers been less healthy, less cared for, or less prepared for life . . . " warned a recent joint report of the Association of School Boards and the American Medical Association. Yet where was there one helping hand, one human voice?

A "professor", and acting editor of a major journal of opinion, simply excused it all, "We've given them access to an adult world. We have to learn to live with the consequences." Such a man could readily have learned to serve Hitler or Stalin.

Comprehension of our world in its tragic turmoil, unseen by so many, must begin with an agreement on and understanding of what it is above all else, that we need or desire: our purpose. There can be no greater tragedy for a person than to lose all purpose in life, but far more catastrophic is for a whole society to lose purposeful guidance, and to gallop madly into disasters like the swine of the Gadarenes. Our pre-human forebears were guided by a purpose externally imposed by God or Nature, to survive -- implacable and unmanipulatable. Under this guidance, the evolution of human society began, gradually developing natural law, families and parental tenderness, ethical education beginning as primitive, tribal "initiation rites" for young males into adulthood (incipient in some animals), and finally attainment of conscious reason and ideas, of religion and science. This great progress was the direct result of a purpose: to survive and to rise up, which led to what we know as human society; our leaders today reject this humanness in their greed for total power.

Ancient man came to realize that a great transition had occurred, a Fall, and they related it to the attainment of reason. Reason was involved but more fundamentally the real problem was loss of purpose. The fall came as knowledge from reasoned experiences gradually allowed men to push back from the edge of an imposed need to survive. Accordingly, some 10,000 years ago as agriculture became intensive in great river valleys, plenty led to population and security; consequently the authority of tribal societies based on survival faded in the affluence and confusion mounted. A clique of intellectuals whose only purpose was total control grabbed power probably through a monopoly on information on how to run the new economy, and gradually the masses were terrorized into a sub-human servitude with threats of "angry gods". Totalitarianism was born, with a bureaucracy, and mass slavery, from Mesopotamia to Meso-America. Innovations were sharply proscribed by the bureaucracy for fear something would get out of hand. Plato noted the frozen nature of Egyptian art.

These god-king empires might still exist today but for human societies such as the Greeks that still struggled on in barren lands to survive, and who came to fear the ancient god-king tyrannies where "Seers bring terror to keep men afraid". It was presumably the intuitive urge from this fear that drove them to fix consciously on a purpose, to guide them by the abyss. To recover from the loss of purpose in the Fall, man would have to impose a new purpose for social guidance upon himself, and to support and maintain it himself with his reason. "It is a preeminent enterprise of any culture to produce the judgment of what is really good and really evil in human life." By thus focusing their efforts on seeking that "proper to man" the Greeks not only defeated a god-king tyranny but created a supreme culture that was to become the foundation for Western civilization. The Christian world followed with an equivalent purpose, to seek the will of God.

However, neither Greeks nor Christians comprehended that an overarching social purpose was essential for social coherence and rational progress, *nor is it today*. These are not suppositions; they constitute recorded history. We know that the Greeks made more progress in 800 years than did the god-king empires in 8,000. Also in some 1,000 years following the fall of Rome it was the work and guidance of the Christian world that transformed Europe from a wilderness of dense forests inhabited by barbarous tribes to a land of towns and farms, cities with canals for transportation, beautiful cathedrals, and universities where reason was used as never before. There was Dante and Shakespeare, and later modern science, freedom in self-government, and an end to slavery.

The great scholar Max Weber a century ago declared that "Western civilization only . . . (had) *universal* significance and value", because "Only in the West" was culture rational. But he didn't explain why it was rational, nor that intellectuals had long been undermining its rationality. Some 400 years ago intellectuals had become aware of a weakening of conviction in the Christian purpose, so Machiavelli advised his colleagues to cease urging restraint on the masses; promise them their fondest dreams and we can again be as gods. The Reasoners promised material plenty from science and urged rejection of religion (and hence purpose) for unshackled reason, thereby abandoning rationality and initiating modernity. The Enlighteners promised release from the bonds of society, for an anomic individualism, for a social being! The liberal-socialists promised release from all "impositions".

The structure of modern totalitarianism was laid out by the French "Economists" in 1755 as described by Tocqueville, who warned that if people allowed the State to usurp all initiatory action, they would gradually slide into a sub-human servitude. Herbert Spencer repeated the warning; Nobelist Albert Schweitzer perceived a "suicide of civilization", and by 1936 Walter Lippmann declared that a new establishment of collectivist "overhead planners" had taken over, subversively albeit. "No other approach considered . . . only a handful here and there . . . isolated and disregarded challenge it". In 1951 British Labor Party spokesman, Barbara Ward, wrote: "The Western experiment . . . really the most audacious and exhilarating of mankind . . . appears on the defensive". "The Western vision fades . . . (with) glimpses of Moloch and Baal, the terrible gods of the State . . . reasserting their ancient sway". How mortally appalling it is that today people fail to resist a second fall from humanness into sub-human servitude.

Western civilization, our civilization that is: "so distinctive and luminous in its character, imposing in its duration, so utterly without rival on the face of the earth", wrote Cardinal Newman well over a century ago, that we give to it "the abstract term 'civilization'." Today any group of people may be awarded the term, and our universities vow its eradication and the media and schools act on that renegadism. No one seems to notice or care.

In America intellectuals have long assured people that there was no socialism here, and Communism posed no danger. But by 1900 a network of socialist cells had been organized in our leading universities, whose mission would be "to go through the institutions" (later named Gramsci's strategy) necessary for an organized society to maintain self government. These were to be taken over and transformed into instruments of Statism: John Dewey and others developed the basis for our now corrupted education; Morris Cohen at Harvard proposed "judicial legislation" to end the rule of law and to justify an intent-less Constitution; Franz Boas and his women at Columbia University initiated a direct assault on Western civilization.

Without the knowledge that the control of public opinions and perceptions was safely in the hands of those favorable to "overhead planning" as Lippmann reported, Franklin Roosevelt would not have dared nor been allowed to bait the Japanese into an attack, nor under the cover of wartime security to ally himself with Stalinism, certainly deemed at that time to be the most evil regime in the world.

He claimed his purpose was to "slaughter Hitler", when Hitler and Stalin were still allies, but his real vision was to empower Communism in Western Europe, and even in America, as Arthur Schlesinger has admitted. "Spasmodically, incompletely, somewhat formlessly, but always in the same direction, inching its ice cap over the nation for decades", wrote Whittaker Chambers in 1952. By 1990, Schlesinger recognized that the inching was nearly compete.

Democracy, equality, and diversity are unnatural,
Poisons to natural society, to that proper to man.

II THE WAR

You can't fix what you don't understand, so understanding the truth about the subversion and despoiling of our self-governing human society is essential. It must not be turned from as too shocking, or rejected as disparaging; truth is often both.

For the past century, a well organized and powerful clique has planned and has been executing a decade-by-decade attack on America and much of the West, on the institutions essential for humanness and self-government. As no greater crime against humanity can be imagined, it is essential to *insist* that the attacking clique be recognized as "renegades" and an "evil regime" by all who would save human society. Failure to denounce evil is the beginning of greater evil. The New World Order and the destruction of Western Civilization are both movements toward global fascism; it cannot possibly be democratic, let alone human.

The core of the clique operates from deep within a media-academia complex, from where it controls public opinion, education, culture, publishing, and hence public perceptions, standards and the awarding of honors and celebrity. It operates as a total regime with control over the bureaucracies both public and private; neither Congress, Court, nor business, dare to go beyond that which it declares to be "mainstream". It was through its guidance that progressive education devastated literacy, our once revered Constitution denied "intent", ending rule-of-law; and families, decency, and humanness were thrown to the winds of change.

In 1987 Allen Bloom declared that "Much of the intellectual machinery . . . (of the century's) political and social science was constructed for the purpose of making an assault" on our culture. In 1952, the eminent Jewish scholar, Lucy Dawidowicz, had accused a clique of liberals -- there were no Communists, remember -- of attempting to use Jews as they had long used blacks in "a war against America".(1)* Former Communist, Eugene Lyons, a Jewish, Russian-born journalist whose eyes had been opened, wrote of the Thirties, "An intellectual and moral red terror spread through . . . New York, Hollywood, Washington, and many college campuses . . . the fullest force . . . was reserved for renegades . . . one time Communist supporters . . ." "Secretly edited Communist 'shop papers' in the *New York Times*, in *Time* Magazine and others made life miserable for bosses. . . (even) for radicals on the staff who were anti-Stalinist".(2) A non-Communist liberal is as much of an oxymoron as an irreligious conservative. These were the people who supported and iconized Alger Hiss and Franklin Roosevelt, who manned the decade-by-decade attacks on our human society, and without whose support Roosevelt would never have been able to sacrifice, knowingly, the lives of thousands of young men to gain entry to the Soviet-German War to save and to empower Communism.

But it must be asked and answered, what difference does it make now? Why bring up old quarrels and denigrate historical figures? We won the war, won the peace, communism is gone; we have come to "the end of history". On the contrary, these questions and statements exemplify the imposed false perceptions and lies that must be undone before objective discussions of today's problems can be held.

We did not win the war, totalitarianism did; it is at the core of the new globalism. We were told in 1939 that we would have to go to war, and a million of us volunteered, to end the idea that the State should tell people how to live. Yet the major result of WW II was the very opposite; the empowerment of Statism around the

* Numbered References

world, and the intensifying of an attack on humanness and civilization, by the media, universities, education, and bureaucracies both public and private.

This book has been written for the very reason that *we did not* win the war, and we lost the "peace". The virulent growth of total Statism, by the efforts of "red diaper" babies,(3) their allies and offspring, has assumed a global goal. The towering victory of inhuman Statism, as exemplified in the success of partial-birth abortions, uninvestigated deaths of high government officials, use of tanks, poisonous gas outlawed in war, with assault helicopters, and 700 "agents" against a small religious compound in Waco and left uninvestigated, with corruption in the media and government, *unrelieved by any significant opposition*, signals a destruction of human society by a total regime. Oh, they say, there is opposition; look at the virulence of recent political struggles. Nonsense, the struggle is for power not a human purpose. There is no Right and Left, only a Fast and a Slow, both bent on the same global Statism. (A confirmation of this statement may be found in *Tragedy and Hope* by so-called Clinton mentor at Georgetown, Carroll Quigley: "replace (the party in power) every four years . . . by the other party . . . pursue(ing) with new vigor . . . the same policies".)

People must be sparked, like an engine; they will respond to a great human purpose, or to the knout of terror. There is no Third Way, as Lenin admitted. Progress, social felicity, literature, art, religion and science are human responses to a deeply held urge to rise up. Politics is the institution of human society for achieving consensual agreements through open and rational discussions, according to an agreed purpose. But when purpose fades the spark decays, bringing anxiety, resentment, anger, even violence.

A child has little comprehension of adjectives, subjunctives and conditionals, but recognizes what they say. Likewise young people have little comprehension of rationality, humanness and society, but are very aware of their absence. When a young person fails to make contact with his culture and "has no chance to identify with anyone or anything, he becomes a nobody, a nothing . . . (as seen) in the despairing emptiness of so many young faces . . . indeed disinherited . . . an enemy of society", warned Nobel ethologist Konrad Lorenz.(4)   So came the violence in middle-class schools.

It is not a political war or a cultural war; it is really not a war at all, for there is little significant opposition to what is in reality a ravaging. Many celebrated "scholars" not only insist that there is no social catastrophe, but meet any suggestion of illegitimacy in this renegade regime with scathing rebuke. Few dare to stand against them or even to discuss their trampling down of our formerly free institutions. And any statement of unwanted fact is met with vehement disparaging of intentions.

Many gambits are used in the regime's control strategies; one noted by Schumpeter: "a guffaw is an excellent method for disposing of an uncomfortable truth". He also explained that "a sneer will serve as well as a refutation", "the average audience (being) unaware (of its) covering the impossibility of denial". A new one has been added: "It depends upon what 'is' is!" Then they widely and loudly raise the media-promoted ridicule of all accusations of evil intent as "conspiracy theory", yet all of these attacks against society and humanness have been conspiratorial -- a joining in collusion to do wrongful or evil acts with contempt for truth since Machiavelli revealed his strategy, and as Lenin agreed.

A most prevalent gambit among intellectuals is a spurious profundity, an erumpent arrogance of theoreticians deconstructing texts, denying truth and standards, while strutting as emperors in their transparent critical theories. Beware of all social theories; society and all of its important institutions were evolved experimentally -- Nature's experiments. Religion, ideally, consists of man's efforts to understand his spiritual needs and the reality of his existence. Church religion, quite different, is man's erring answers and teachings. Similarly for America, our native land is a "City on a Hill" which people have worked to improve even as they struggled and died for it. The intellectual's "evil Amerika" and "racist America" are but frothings of bigoted renegades. If there were a better place they'd be there.

III THE DEMONIC DREAM

Nor can you control what you don't understand. Today misunderstandings and deceptions corrupt much of our "mainstream's" imposed perceptions. "It's not what people don't know, it's what they know that tain't so". Recovery from our slide into Statism must begin with gaining a general comprehension of how we got where we are, the nature of human society, of its guidance in culture, and how to recover from the usurpation of Statism. A noted writer recently "explained" how we got here, claiming it happened in the 70s; this totally miscomprehends the catastrophic depth of the abyss into which we slide. Comprehension requires a desire to know and a willingness to work and study with an open mind. Be aware that the meaning of words and uncontested terms, so essential for rational discussions of social problems, have been everywhere corrupted.

This war against humanity had its origin in a demonic dream, that invaded the consciousness of Western intellectuals some 400 years ago. Machiavelli perceived that by promising a utopia, intellectuals could capture people's minds and become as gods. With the fading of the power of the church their regime would be unopposed, and so the Economists planned modern totalitarianism in 1755, according to Tocqueville.(1) Today Statism in America has no significant opposition. The core of the regime's power lies in a media-academia complex, from where an elite is able to control public opinions and perceptions. Congress, Court, and bureaucracy will do only what the "mainstream" media will support; without significant opposition the regime is in essence totalitarian. It may be argued that the attacks on human society since Machiavelli's time were not the result of his demonic dream, but it would be a delusion to suppose that intellectuals have not been influenced by its warrant.

"Government" is that human enterprise created by free people, and subservient to them, for enforcing laws and protecting their social order; "laws" clearly imply a self-government under law. A "regime" imposes order not by law but by dictates -- executive or bureaucratic orders; thus a "regime" is totally different from government and must be distinguished by an appropriate name. When a Constitution is denied "intent", that authority has not disappeared, it has been grabbed, purloined by a regime. It is no accident that these concepts have been confounded in today's education and mainstream. The corruption of language is a major tactic of liberalism.

Politics is the institution of a self-governing human society for achieving social guidance through consensual discussions and compromises. Rational discussions are critically dependent upon standards being observed for word meanings and long accepted uncontested terms, and especially upon a first responsibility to an over-arching purpose for guiding self-government and humanness. True political discussions today have been replaced by media-imposed perceptions of an ideology as enforced by a bureaucracy. Like morality, politics exists only in self governed human societies. Rational discussions, if they occur at all in a regime, can exist only among the very top leaders, and even there their purpose is basically different from that of a society.

When people are deprived of the power to hold discussions for making laws for their community, that power does not disappear. It is grasped by men more voraciously than gold, striven for and taken by the most ruthless. The transfer of power to a regime was forced in Russia and China by revolutionary terror. In America and much of the West the transfer has been nearly achieved gradually through dissembling, lies, intimidation and subversion: *Conspiracy.*

The ultimate disaster, however, is not the demonic dream of unrestrained totalitarian power. Rather, as people lose freedom of independent action, they gradually slide into a sub-humanness, as Tocqueville warned. Evidence for the fatal decay is everywhere: in homes, schools, law courts, media, "entertainment", even in churches, and in increasing violence, indecencies, and indifference. It is a known fact, so evidenced in the past century, that people gradually become "comfortable" with obscenities, promiscuities, corruption, violence, filth and inhumanness, and one of these promotes the others. "Use can almost change the very stamp of nature." Our slipping into that abyss must be stopped quickly before it becomes irreversible. Recovery must start with an organized effort to reestablish an *intent* to recover our human society. It must begin with the rebuilding of new channels for discussion of issues and planning, that are independent of the current regime. Truth in a human purpose will provide motivation for action that can bring new meaning to people's lives.

"We lack any kind of historical perspective, any perception of why our country is the way it is . . .", was the recent plea of a young writer in a major journal.(2) "Never before has a generation been less healthy, less cared for, or less prepared for life . . . ", was charged jointly by the American Medical Association and the Association of School Boards. "We no longer care what happens to them". "Individually and collectively we are losing control of the forces that control our lives", was the warning of M. J. Sandel.(3) All people, but particularly young people, should recognize the decadence of so much around them as a major reinforcement of these warnings.

A measure of the misinformation and irrationality is evidenced in the rejection of "impositions". "Don't push your culture, morality, or religion on me!" My God, life is an imposition, as is family, school, hunger, even survival. The "impositions" which are commonly complained of are, however, the standards for living cooperatively and peacefully in a human society. These are the standards of natural law for non-aggression and altruism within a society, essential for social stability; the standards of language, grammar, uncontested terms, and truth essential for the serious discussions necessary for self-government, and standards for humanness, decency, responsibility and honor for families of human beings. Who would question the need for prospective athletes or musicians to accept many impositions in discipline, standards, and personal responsibility to facilitate their progress? However, the challenge to seek to be a human being in a human society requires far more effort, and the rewards for success and penalties for failure are greater than for all else. Humanness evolved out of a long and tumultuous struggle, imposed on our forebears to survive and to rise up. It is not a given; it must be taught and striven for, and failure even to try has been the main factor in the terrible violence and indecencies in today's homes, communities, and government.

It is *purpose*, any purpose, that demands impositions, creates right and wrongs, and purpose is the conforming principle upon which all rationality depends. When you come to an intersection, there is obvious truth as to the right way to turn to be conformable with previous turns and as determined by where you want to go -- your purpose.(4) This compatibility is the essence of rationality; purposes forces an additivity of effects of successive efforts, enabling progress.

What the earnest young man, who protested the "lack of a historical perspective", needs is to know who he is, to have a human purpose that alone can give his life meaning, and to possess some recognition of the nature of humanness and the forces that are destroying it. The "historical perspective" that is needed is of human society, what it is, how and why it has been nearly destroyed by demonic dreamers, and especially how to recover. "To have his path made clear to him is the aspiration of every human being." The path urged by Machiavelli and followers is downwards to subservience; that offered by the great writers of Western civilization is upwards towards that "proper to man".

It is a basic ethological principle that nearly everything that people do is commanded or urged by innate behavioral programs. In the physical world there are the innate urges for food, protection, and sex, while in man's spiritual world of feelings there are urges to belong to some communion, to obey conscience, and deepest of all to rise up: "to know" claimed the philosopher; "to admire", "to admire the better . . .

the taproot of civilization", wrote the poet. But what we *do* in response to these urges is necessarily reasoned, for it must be guided according to site and situation-specific conditions known only to reason; the nature-nurture controversy is a misunderstanding, both are needed. Hence the great importance of education and culture, for we can only reason from what we know.

Young people we are told won't accept "impositions"; they want rap-rock, junk food, and to do their own thing. This is obvious nonsense; if young people were to hear from birth only good music, have only healthful food at regular set meals and given a proper attitude toward responsibility, discipline, and a joy in learning, they would find the rap rock, junk food and TV loathsome. They need to be taught that purpose determines all things, beginning with truth. How glorious, to pursue human greatness with hope and joy, for all who will try.

"Righteousness is what is loved."
The beginning of humanness and spiritual life,
A 5000 year old Egyptian inscription.

ADDENDUM:

Three additional warnings of the decline and disintegration of Western civilization must be noted: C.S. Lewis' *Abolition of Man* (containing "Men Without Chests") in 1947, and R.M. Weaver's *Ideas Have Consequences*, and C.F. M. Joad's *Decadence*, in 1948. Weaver's book has been read more widely, but Joad's is deeper philosophically and Lewis' the most spiritual. All three insisted that civilization rested on recognition and support for that in man which rises beyond the animal and the material, which Aristotle described as "far above all the rest".

IV THE SUPREME QUESTION

To those seeking to be human beings, nothing is more important than their society and its guidance in culture. Societies have strength only if organized (under a purpose, for an organization without purpose is an oxymoron), and depend upon that social order for survival, man no less then bees in their hive, wolves in their pack, or birds in a flock. Yet modern writers almost completely ignore the concept of society, and culture so essential for its guidance is corrupted to little more than a political straw-man.

Even the scholar, Allen Bloom, wrote, "I have no understanding of what culture is . . . a word I never use . . . extremely difficult to discern."(1) He was confused or confounded because he lacked an understanding of "society"; it is absent from his writings. Culture has real importance only as guidance for a human society; without society, culture is like a man without purpose, leaves in the wind, a dummy like Bloom's decadent university.

Societies are organized collectives, provided by Nature or God to effect cooperative survival. The spirit of a society is most profoundly exhibited in the powerful communal honking of a "triumph ceremony" of Konrad Lorenz's greylag geese, wherein was heard millions of years ago the first *Hallelujah Chorus*, declaring a belonging to a communion and a celebration of that which is felt. Bloom did quote Nietzsche: "a shared sense of the sacred is the surest way to recognize a culture". It is society, however, that is sacred, as in totemism from which all major religions evolved.

Society is sacred, meaning most precious for survival, because it is *the organization* that maintains social *order*, without which there will be unbearable chaos, from which only terror can regain peace. Society is precious like the "us" of a small band in very desperate surroundings, sacred like family. Society is an organization of "We the People", held together by the bonds of need and belonging, that makes freedom and self-government possible. Society will fail if the bonds decline and order collapses; only in a society will humanness be maintained, as we see in all the collapsed societies around the world which have been so readily taken over by tyrannical regimes.

Society as the supreme organization for humanness in self government is little emphasized in Western literature. The Greek *polis* was the remnant of their prehistoric tribal society. In the Christian world the Church recreated a human organization within the Roman Empire, and for much of two millennia provided the organization for human society. The great corruption of modernism was not so much that intellectuals effectively destroyed religion, although in a deeper sense perhaps it was; the immediate and pressing disaster has been the absence, with its removal, of any significant, organized attempt to maintain a structure for humanness. This may have resulted from ignorance or oversight for awhile, but is unbelievable for five centuries, and particularly as inhumanness mounted in the past century.

Standing above society must be a purpose, much like God Himself as Scotus declared, which defines truth, bestows rationality, implements order, enables progress, and justifies social impositions and restraints. Thus the truth of the right way to turn at an intersection depends on where you want to go, your purpose. And purpose provides the guiding force that induces a conformability among successive turns, which is the essence of rationality and progress.

A Social Contract, imposed by God or Nature, defined the first social order for our forebears some seven million years ago, as a strategy for more certain survival. In return for protection, fellowship, and the mystic bonds of belonging, our forebears accepted the impositions of natural law, with required altruism and social responsibility. This social order created the domain of society, wherein humanness was nurtured until, guided by a purpose to seek that "proper to man", it became a reasoning human society; only therein would an organized effort to maintain it be the supreme purpose, to be taught, exemplified and celebrated in a culture. Without the support and protection of an organized society, all humanness becomes contingent, a mere forbearance of usurpers, leaving only inhumanness.

Primitive societies were guided in large issues of survival by a tribal Council of Elders, while "all that concerns the lives, liberties and properties of the people" was fixed largely by custom, and by discussions leading to consensual agreements -- the true origin of self governing human societies. Society first broke down some 10,000 years ago when affluence from reasoned advances, particularly intensive agriculture in great river valleys, undermined the tribal social order which was dependent upon the purpose of survival for authority. From Mesopotamia to Meso-America cliques of intellectuals grabbed power in the confusion, and terrorized the people into a sub-human servitude with threats of "angry gods". They created a bureaucratic totalitarianism, the first Statism, with mass slavery, taught superstitions, corrupted "religion" in a total regime, unrestrained by any internal force or external need.

These ancient god-king tyrannies were defeated by a tribal human society of free men, the Greeks, who lived beyond the easy reach of a bureaucratic Statism. Recognizing, presumably intuitively, a need for a purposed social-guidance to supplement the fading force of survival, they began to focus their social efforts by seeking that "proper to man", perhaps as an intuitive, fear-driven means for avoiding the seen abyss of a tyrannical Statism's bureaucracy, where "Seers bring terror to keep men afraid." Fear wonderfully concentrates the mind, as Dr. Johnson noted.

It is important to emphasize that in primitive pre-agricultural societies, purpose as survival was imposed, externally and unmanipulatable, upon people. When the need to struggle to survive became no longer an implacable and constant necessity, choices became possible. It was the supreme gift of the Greeks to Western civilization to have provided a self-imposed, internal purpose, to guide these choices to humanness to a rising up to that "proper to man". This led to something new and revolutionary, only vaguely recognized today. Culture as knowledge through reasoned experiences in the physical world had long existed, even among some animals. The Greeks made it into something entirely new; now culture would support a new spiritual world, as an explication and celebration of that "proper to man" -- humanness -- and become the basis for that which alone should be recognized as civilization. The cause or origin of the need for such an overarching purpose, to guide social rationality, was not recognized by the Greeks, *nor is it today.*

Nor is the need for maintaining an elite, to nurture, to implement, and to advance the purpose of humanness as a base for social rationality and truth. The Supreme Question is how to give to an elite power over social guidance, and yet keep them from destroying human society and declaring themselves rulers. Peculiarities in the Greek *polis* provided them temporarily with such an elite; then in the Christian world the Church came to stand as the restraining force for moderating tyranny, for bringing freedom, literature, art and science, universities, ending slavery, and for providing social guidance.

But elite, order, organization, and purpose are all insignificant without an inner feeling, a *conviction*. Communists, alone in all the world, Whittaker Chambers found, had retained "the power to hold convictions and to act on them".(2) Today people must be convinced of the supreme need to retain humanness: "Recreate for your age the vision of Man".

The majority of people are kept busy surviving, with work and families. They seldom possess the knowledge, the time, or the inclination to deal with many social problems, however they are very capable of sensing when a proposed policy will be destructive of freedom or humanness; that is their principal function in self-government. Today nearly every major policy of the regime: on education, quotas, abortion, immigration, law, and families, is opposed by a significant majority of citizens, yet they have no voice. Only intellectual leaders are capable of guiding society effectively, but they will be tempted to turn renegade when they see unopposed power available to them. Sixteenth century Machiavelli, perceived that the power of the Church was fading and saw the opportunity. Cease urging restraint on the commons, he advised his intellectual colleagues; promise them their fondest dreams and they will follow us as gods. So promises were the bait of the Reasoners, and of the Enlighteners, the Liberals and the socialists; the demonic dream. Now again we see a bureaucratic clique gaining unrestrained power in America, with promises and fear becoming the means for obtaining compliance.

Ancient totalitarianism, noted previously, long predates modernity, and it is enlightening to note the parallels. An appalling hiatus, in humanness, of some 8000 years, came into existence as would be expected, between the pre-agricultural human society of natural man and the subsequent human society and culture of the Greeks. Natural man in a moderate environment was not Hobbesian, "poor, nasty and brutish". He was exuberant, free and doing. We see him in early tribal Greeks, plains Indians, in the Paleolithic cave artist of the "Wild Horse of Montespan" of 15,000 years ago, searching for something beyond; as the art critic Fauré felt in Constable's landscapes, "I am the Resurrection and the Life". The artists of the maidens of LaMadelaine, "portrayed the human form thousands of years in advance" of the later art of god-king empires, according to Van Doren Stern.(3) Leakey noted "techniques of perspective and movement reinvented (only) with the Renaissance".(4)

This hiatus in man's spiritual world of art and feelings under ancient Statisms, was matched by a similar stultification in material progress. Innovations were proscribed for fear something might get out of hand -- early Lysenkoism. Plato noted the frozen nature of Egyptian art. The Greeks made more progress in 800 years than did the god-king empires in

8000 with vastly more facilities and time. And the humanly-purposed Christian world continued the miraculous progress in humanness for over one thousand years after the fall of Rome. But then its human purpose started slowly to decay; only science which retained a guiding purpose, a search for truth, continued to progress, but even that is faltering now.

Another hiatus in humanism is thus obviously developing, becoming noticeable after Samuel Johnson and smothering all humanness since WW I. Nietzsche predicted it, and Tocqueville warned that if the State was allowed to grasp all initiatory power the people would gradually fall into a subhumanness.(5) Nobelist Albert Schweitzer(6) saw the suicide of civilization coming, and Walter Lippmann in 1936 warned of Statists "undoing the work of emancipation, the steps men have taken to limit the power of rulers".(7) British Labor Party "spokesman" and scholar, Barbara Ward, wrote in 1951, "The Western experiment . . . really the most audacious and exhilarating of mankind . . . appears on the defensive . . . The Western vision fades . . . (with) glimpses of Moloch and Baal, the terrible gods of the State . . . reasserting their ancient sway".(8) In a global order there will no longer be outsiders, such as the Greeks, to regain humanness.

The greatest crime against humanity has been the methodical, assiduous, decade-by-decade struggle by intellectuals to subvert, to uproot, and to destroy humanness and the society that has made it possible. The people of the "mainstream" party who have guided this subversion are responsible for this great crime and must be recognized as renegades, the lowest order of traitors, the most detestable enemies of their own people. Hatred should not refer to behavior that is politically or culturally incited within a society; today too often hatred along with contempt are simulated or imposed as perceptions. Properly hatred is an innate feeling; no more eradicable than hunger. Contempt is proper for people who do shameful things within their society. Hate is innately proper for renegades who have put themselves outside of their society, as external enemies who seek to subvert and to destroy all humanness for a whole people.

Young people are exposed in schools to the grossest indecencies and perversions, when they should be learning of their culture; they are exposed to the most inhuman brutalities and demonic violence in entertainment instead of confident and human discipline; they see cheats, liars, scoundrels, courtesans and vicious criminals and perverts celebrated and enriched. Much that is civilized, decent and honorable is stigmatized, denigrated and ridiculed. Those who deny the deepening horrors of our society help its destroyers.

Culture, families, rule of law, and education in right and wrong are essential for providing order and guidance in a human society. Statism needs none of these, for all guidance and order are provided by the bureaucratic State; "culture" becomes mere entertainment, as sports, infantility, and the erotic. We can see growing here and now, the horror of inhuman Statism.

For much of two millennia, the human societies of the West were guided by the Christian churches. They decided much of law, provided festivals for socializing and relaxation, held the weekly ear of the common people, and educated the elite. Most art, literature and music was created for an explication and celebration of Christian purpose, setting the tone and goals for the "moral education of the people". Even the French Revolution in taking over the Louvre Palace dedicated it as a museum for that purpose. Liberal J.S. Mill(9) inanely complained that the power of religion existed not so much in itself as in its power over public opinion. Whom do you suppose he thought should have that power, and for what purpose?

Most all behavior is as urged or commanded by innate behavioral programs, to answer physical demands, and the spiritual needs to belong and to rise up, but it is reason guided by custom and taught in culture that determines the response. Hence people must be taught, the innate and the cultural, as young robins are taught. J.S. Mill(10) defined culture as "that knowledge which one generation gives to its successors for at least keeping up, if not raising . . . ", in humanness.

The fatuosity is often heard that "rock-rap is what young people like and want". "The old taboos are dying . . . nudity, obscene language, candid lyrics, erotic art . . . People are breaking the bonds of puritan society and helping America to grow up." Asinine when published by *Newsweek* in 1967. "This revolution has been made by young people and nothing will thwart it . . . the truth will out . . . strip away the sham and cant of their elders", David Susskind. People want that which is familiar and celebrated; they cannot want what they never see or hear, as good music, a reverence for humanness, and respect for excellence and the honorable. Children enjoy to play and to make noise naturally, as do animals, but to learn good music, to read with discernment, and to comprehend humanness requires education, an understanding of excellence, and a joy in rising up. The inhumanness which has been pushed on to the people for much of a century, is now claimed to be "what people want."

Michael Oakeshott followed Nietzsche in asserting that "education begins when a human inheritance of feelings, beliefs, understandings, and activities supervenes on momentary desires and imaginings." All things *must be taught*, directly or by exemplified custom. If young people heard only good music from birth to twelve years of age, rock-rap would be abominable, as today the rock-rappers reject good music. Today's "progressive" education is not only a shameful thing; in spite of many good people it has been the most effective tool of the renegade clique in the destruction of education for self government, and in the uprooting of human society and Western civilization. Increasing the vast money flow to them makes them more effective destroyers.

The great scholar Max Weber declared that "Western civilization only . . . (has) *universal* significance and value",(11) because "Only in the West" was culture rational. But its rationalizing purpose had long before come under attack with Machiavelli, then the Reasoners, the Enlighteners, Liberals and then the Communist-Statists. Weber wrote, as the 20th century was beginning, before WW I, before the New Deal (recognized as near-fascist at the time), before WW II and especially before the Sixties. Today nearly every effort of media, government, foundations, and the entire "mainstream" is to destroy rational culture and to give more power to the State while despoiling families, education, rule of law and self government.

The Supreme Question of humanity asks, how can a society maintain guidance for a self-governing human society, for civilization? That is best done by a designated elite. However, the common people are very capable of recognizing policies destructive of human society and its supports in families, education, rule of law and purposed social coherence. They are, unfortunately, readily swayed by self-interest, bordering on greed. The "modest parson", Shakespeare's and almost Machiavelli's peer, Richard Hooker, wrote, "He that goeth about to persuade a multitude that they are not so well off as they ought to be, shall never want attentive and favorable hearers." Promises, promises! Machiavelli had marked the way.

Nations are coming apart, around the world, breaking up into ethnicities: the Soviet Union, the British nation, the Balkans, Africa, Middle East and now America. The ethnicity of peoples who constructed Western civilization was until WW I commonly referred to as Aryan. It was a name of sufficient dignity and respect that socialists, particularly the Marx-Engels socialists, originated "Aryan superiority" to gain adherents, and it was from them that Hitler appropriated the concept. No one hyperventilates over "God's Chosen People", or the "Flowery Kingdom:, or other self-congratulatory names. "Aryan superiority" was an appropriated vestment to cloak socialism's inhumanness. Now the very word "Aryan" has been proscribed as sharply as "nigger", but Western civilization is Aryan, as has largely been the Christian world and most of today's freedom and science. The word is now exploited as part of the effort to stigmatize, even to criminalize, the concept of Western civilization and its founders. Nobel ethologist Konrad Lorenz wrote that the commonality of body language exhibited during major social rituals for all peoples around the world, evidenced a once-common culture.(12) It is accordingly even more reasonable to insist that all people speaking an Aryan-related (or Sanskrit-related) European language, evolved from a more recent common culture.(13) There is great potential power in realizing such a belonging, and that is the essence of what the renegade "mainstream" seeks to stigmatize. Clearly we are entering an era in which only your ethnicity and culture will offer you protection, civility and fidelity.

The question is how to support an elite attentive to the needs of a people of a self-governing human society, and to the advancement of a positive culture for guidance thereto. How to honor and support them, yet keep them from subverting policies to facilitate their own demonic dream of god-hood. The Christian churches did it quite well for much of two millennia, to the great advantage of the world. It is a complex question to consider, but first a clearer understanding of humanness is needed. This will aid in comprehending that the struggle today is not about capitalism, socialism, liberalism, racism, bigotry, or conservatism. It is very simply a matter of regaining a self governing human society -- there is no other kind -- or sinking into a sub human servitude to modern pyramid builders who would be as gods. Martin Malia like many other scholars has suggested that "a desire for a utopia" has been the cause for many intellectuals to cling to Communism. Perhaps for the "Lenin's idiots" but certainly not for the leaders, they fully comprehend their goal; democracy and equality, their major tools along with non-judgmentalism and diversity, are unnatural, destructive of society and humanness. Any doubts of such intentions can be quenched by reading the last chapter of Jean Baudrillard's *Amérique* (Fr.), or J.W. Ceaser's account in *Reconstructing America*, in postmodernism.(14)

After a brief note on the Aryans, a more detailed examination of human society will prepare the way to an answer to the Supreme Question.

A REMINDER:

The exact definition, as applied to the word "culture", is of little significance relative to the *idea*: that there does exist a body of knowledge, "That one generation gives to its successors for rising up" in humanness. So too for the words religion and truth; these ideas must be taught, with honored names, in seeking to be human. Some of that which is taught as "culture" is not even human.

NOTE ON ARYANS

Over four thousand years ago a great outflow of people began from the Northern Euro-Asian plain. Perhaps thousands of years of struggle to survive along the edge of the glacial icecap may have induced an eugenic imperative, stripped out the weak and nurtured a social order which on retreat of the ice led to a massive population growth. Tribes moved southward into India as a warrior and ruling class, and provided the name Aryan, the Sanskrit language, the *Upanishads*, and the *Bhagavad Gita*.

Nothing makes for a common people more than a common language and culture. In 1767 the French Jesuit Coeurdoux, and later in 1786, Britisher Sir. Wm. Jones, after a lengthy stay in India, noted that Latin and Greek bore a "strange affinity (to Sanskrit), both in root of verbs and form of grammar, than possible by accident -- no philologist could have failed to believe them to have sprung from a common source". All European languages thus belonged to a common culture with Sanskrit. Only a couple of examples will be considered. There is *bruder* in German and *frater* in Latin; Sanskrit is in between, *bhratar*. There are common words for *mead*, for *wagon*, *wheel*, and *axle*, but not for "spoke", suggesting solid wheels. *Wand* in English means "slender rod", but in German it is "wall", suggesting wattle huts with a "wind's eye" or "window". All Aryan languages have words for wolf, beech, and snow, but none has a word for sea. For much of a century "philology" was essentially defined as the "digging for Sanskrit roots", to reveal the common Aryan culture.(1)

Perhaps sometime after 2000 BC other Aryans who had migrated south into the Danube Basin began to filter into what is now Greece. They created the Parthenon and the ideas basic to Western civilization and freedom. Others moved into Italy where they developed the Latin world, and the basic concepts of Western law and government. The Celts and later the Teutons swept across Europe to the Western verge, and after stopping momentarily, continued on to a New World, on to the Antipodes and poles. Finally to the Moon. There was Dante and DaVinci, the Schoolmen, Shakespeare, Kant, and modern science. Yes, there were borrowings, from Semites, Chinese and Hindus, and American Indians. But the concept and guiding force was Aryan. It is a heritage upon which we should not pride ourselves so much as to strive to live up to. Today Aryan has been denigrated by the mainstream to a malignity, not just the word "Aryan" but the very concept of humanness and civilization which brought forth the ideas of progress and freedom.

"Those who do not show anger at what shames them are fools", and "to those who let things happen to them, worse will come". For some time now our Census Bureau has knowingly jeered Aryans (or if you will European-Americans) as "non-Hispanic whites"; "non-Semitic whites" is becoming common in the "mainstream"; we become contemptible "nons". Try using "non-Arabic Semites", or "non-Nigerian Africans".

The noted British historian, V. Gordon Childe, published an excellent account of *The Aryans* in 1987. The word Aryan had become as unmentionable as "nigger" or "kike", both rather self given names, after about 1930 in America. Childe however, favored the name in preference to Indo-European -- "clumsy and not scientific" -- as having "advantage of brevity and familiarity".

The "growth of reasoning goes hand-in hand with development of language"; through philology "man has raised himself from savagery to barbarism -- to civilization". It was the "delicate linguistic structure" that accounts for the speakers of this language "outstripping the Ancient East". And it was their "community of speech . . . as a feasible instrument of thought", which promoted a "spiritual unity".

The first great advances towards abstract natural science were made by Aryan Greeks and Hindus, not Babylonians or Egyptians. The first religions to appeal to all men irrespective of race, in a moralization of religion in Buddhism and Zoroastrianism, were Aryan in Aryan speech. The latter may have "even anticipated the Hebrews in sublimating the idea of divinity", emancipating it from tribal rituals.

Childe is an outstanding historian and his ideas cannot be sneered away as "Aryan superiority". An important point is that those who do so are the same people who denigrate human society and Western civilization, and are to be discounted and ignored accordingly.

"All on a razor's edge it stands, either woeful ruin or life." It has been evil leaders that have led Western peoples into a sub human servility.

White people, Aryans, have intentionally been stripped of their protective racial consciousness, as the world moves into a weakening of all protections, national or religious. No where is this more brutally real than in prisons; a warden testifying at a rare "prison rape" trial -- estimated 140,000 annual rapes, nearly all unrecorded -- "it is the prisoner's own responsibility to fight off sexual abuse", as reported in leftist Human Rights Watch's book, *No Escape*.(3) But whites are heavily outnumbered in most prisons by blacks and by Hispanics, even among guards and prison officials who rarely bother to hide their virulently racist hatred.

The stripping of racial consciousness from whites is a reality. Among whites essentially only hardened criminals will cooperate for their own protection, while blacks or Mexicans will riot or fight to the death to protect their own. "Psychosocially, emotionally, physically, the most dangerous and traumatic experience is the open-barracks prison." Whites must choose between repeated gang rapes by blacks, or fighting continually close to death, or becoming sex slaves to a big black, so *No Escape* reported. "I had to submit to becoming a wife (a ho, to avoid the struggle, ripping and tearing of gang rapes) . . . sucking his dick, being fucked in the ass, other duties of a woman . . . making his bed, cleaning his clothes, being loaned out or rented." "When I'm ready to get my freak (sex), no arguments, or else. Do we understand?" For you or your son? That the "mainstream" would not tolerate such evil against Jews or black for one day, is clear evidence of its hatred of whites and their civilization.

V SIMPLE HUMANNESS

For ages our forebears struggled to survive; and a bit more, to rise up towards a humanness, something "proper to man". The essential instruments used were: language as communicability, culture as knowledge acquired from reasoned experiences and passed on to offspring, and operational reason for the generation of rational responses to communications from the environment. Today as the very concept of humanness is ignored, excluded and attacked, and violence, corruption and indifference mount, an examination of its nature and function is needed. The only real "human right" is the right to live in a human society; without which everything is contingent, a mere forbearance; with it all humanness is possible.

The first instrument, a primitive language, served survival for mobile life half a billion years ago. Encoding was in rituals or acting-outs, as a mating ritual, supplemented later with gestures. Even today the most profound social messages, around the world and at all levels of culture, are and always have been encoded in rituals. And gestures and facial expressions are the determined encodings for our deepest messages of passion and compassion. These are conformable with syntactic encoding since all are but data for a basic "cognitive program" for communicability which began with life itself

The second instrument, culture, like truth and science as similarly containing imperfections, was, until the Sixties, always positive knowledge for rising up in a humanness. "Culture gave to (early) *Homo sapiens* a decisive advantage, an opportunity for the future", declared a prominent sociologist.(1) Where is the "opportunity" in much of today's "culture"? J.S. Mill had defined culture for a large audience of university students and professors as "knowledge which one generation gives to its successors for at least keeping up, if not raising", to a humanness.(2) But the Sixties' "counterculture" forced the perception that culture was but behavior, neither good nor bad. Thus the very idea and possibility of humanness was foreclosed and abandoned, replaced by multiculturalism as a precursor for Statism as global fascism. Statism has no need for culture, as it derives its guidance from an ideology.

Recognition of contradictions led to the concept of untruth, and then to truth; the unnatural required a natural, and so too inhumanness determines a humanness as the purpose of culture. Without natural law, fixed truth and an objective nature for man with a purpose to rise up as Mill insisted, everything becomes mere preference. But when you come to an intersection, the *truth* about the right way to turn, depends upon where you want to go, your purpose. Without a purpose it makes no difference; there is no truth nor rationality. The Comte de Sade's rollicking deduction was that without purpose "nothing is forbidden". He failed to mention that unpurposed imagination would lead to a social chaos in which nothing rational would be possible nor would progress. Any game has rules; culture is knowledge that must be learned about the game of human life, along with its ineffable possibilities. Morality, customs, and responsibility should be perceived not as impositions, but as means for rising up in humanness, for playing the game and winning.

The third instrument, operational reason, came as a part of a "cognitive program" which marks the origin of life. Life began not with an ability of a structure to absorb and to utilize energy and information as science claims; first must have come an ability to communicate with the environment, and thus to discover their presence. An interaction with the environment is a two step process, cognition and response. The cognitive program has, of necessity, three *operational* parts: an awareness (consciousness) of patterns in the environment, a storage (memory) for known patterns, and a facility (operational reason) for judging the adequacy of a match between an incident and a known pattern, for example for nutrients, and also for judging the response. The identification of a match constitutes the absorption of information by communication, initiatory to a response.

Nearly all learning and science depend on pattern matching. Metaphors are syntactic patterns. See Lorenz, Ref. 3, p. 24.

The ability to receive site-specific information and to formulate a rational response is essential for all life, including plants. It came into being with the cognitive program whose creation made all life possible. Operational reason required for pattern-match determinations, as for nutrients, is also necessary in the response phase to make "local adjustments" according to site-specific parameters, such as size, distance, orientation, location, and so on, even if the response is an innate behavioral program, as an acting out, or ritual, for absorbing nutrients. You can actually observe such situation-specific behavior of jellyfish off the coast of Georgia, which appear as an on-end beige balloon. When circled, its body will twist as it obviously seeks to follow your movement, though as a jellyfish it lacks all organs, being little more than a collection of cells. It is as though it contained a kind of stem cells, capable of sensing and cognitive powers, as did first life, and extensive like the sense of touch.

For sexual reproduction in mobile species, as early arthropods, the reasoned response to a pattern-match for a possible mate called for the initiation of a "message", as a mating acting-out or ritual. Identification of a competitor provoked an "aggressive display" ritual, with judging (reason) required as to the loser and how to respond accordingly.

Note how easily reasoned "local adjustments" could so naturally add gestures to the ritual acting-outs. Then sounds could be added, as squeaks, grunts and so on; recent research has determined that the complexity of rodent communications by squeaks to be far greater than formerly imagined. Finally how naturally squeaks, growls, grunts and purrs, could lead to verbs. We still growl, grunt and purr. Advances by local adjustments would not depend on slow and chancy mutations, and how like the unfolding of a design, with a jerky evolution. (Note: It is assumed that a series of mutations produced the acting-out encoded message, but that required reasoning, as do nearly all responses. Once reason is guiding the acting-out there is no obvious reason why it could not include the gestures in the act, as reasoned "local adjustments". See Ref. 3A)

Syntactic language is completely conformable with the primitive language, which is still used for much basic social communication. For a child to learn Chinese (a cultural program) instead of English, requires but different data for a basic computer program. Two general ethological principles are exemplified here. First, phylogenetic commands are commonly answered by a *reasoned* response, even if reason chooses an innate motor program. Second, reasoned, cultural rituals or programs tend to be interwoven into innate programs as effectuators, such as the syntactic encoding for the cognitive program, and morality added to natural law. Thus, "Reason panders to will."

These concepts may be clarified by considering the results of Eibl-Eibesfeldt's experiment of a number of years ago. Movies were made showing the gestures and facial expressions of the most widely differing peoples as they performed standard social rituals: greeting, parting, quarreling, and so on. Movies were taken of Australian aborigines, Upper Orinoco Indians, Kalahari Bushmen, Americans and cultured Europeans. Nobel ethologist Konrad Lorenz wrote, "even in slow motion the (gestures and facial expressions) . . . proved to be identical".(3) Since these peoples had been separated for perhaps over 40,000 years, the filmed rituals had to be innate by virtue of their tremendous resistance to change; accompanying cultural rituals as words and gifts exchanged varied widely. Reason necessarily coordinated both the innate and the cultural according to the occasion and site. Human innateness thus provides the common foundation for all cultures, around the world. Nearly all behavior is urged by innate (biological) commands, but the behavioral response is normally executed by reason (culturally).

Hence the nature-nurture controversy is a

misunderstanding; all social behavior involves both, and thereby teaching is so critically important. Simple life, such as wasps, survives nearly totally by following innate behavioral programs, as for nest building which they do though never having seen it done. All common functions: mating, nesting, protecting, eating, are performed "ritually", according to innate programs. Higher animals can learn innate rituals by imitation, and add cultural enhancements; young rats accordingly can learn to avoid certain poisons. Such knowledge, originating from reasoned experiences, becomes vast and complex in still higher primates, and man evolved with an ability to teach consciously to young their culture for survival. Innate commands requiring reasoned responses which must be taught is the universal pattern.

Our forebears' long climb to humanness is marked by three significant turnings. The first and of most importance was a condensation into an interdependent association, a "society", as a strategy for survival, some seven million years ago. Bipedalism may have been promoted by cooperative social activities, as certainly was an expanded cortex. "Parental tenderness", common to higher animals and from which "springs generosity, gratitude, pity, and love", was consciously fostered, and allied with the anger arising from harm to young gave rise to all moral indignation. In fact all that we think of as characteristically human was evolved and nurtured in primitive society: natural law, families, education in ethics, art, self government, and consciousness itself with religion, culture and the idea of progress as rising up. Note the tenacity of the innate.

As reason became more influential nature began to apply restraints as imposed responsibilities. Society was made stable by collateral constraints of non-aggression and altruism *within* the society through natural law, thereby
originating the powerful and innate "us-them" dichotomy. Thus slavery of aliens was not prohibited, but fornication, violence and all things destructive of families and social peace were. Into these innate roots which had to be taught

through reason, were interwoven cultural effectuators producing morality and charity, and reason became responsible for social coherence. "Individual" morality is almost an oxymoron. People define words to suit their purpose; if the purpose is to understand humanness then words must be found to fit the controlling concepts. For the functioning of a human society the innate programs for interdependent survival must effect social behavior, and the cultural effectuators of significance must be those concepts or practices held in common by the society.

Perhaps two million years ago, Nature began invoking a most powerful restraint on reason by gradually assigning to males the responsibility for the care of a female and *their* offspring, as a family. This has never been total, but the violence of male aggression was greatly reduced, and it provided an extended period of protection and training for young males of families to absorb an expanding culture. These families would have provided the tribal leaders, and become the building blocks and essential training centers for a human society. They can and must again.

It may have been soon afterwards that primitive "initiation rites" into adulthood, incipient in some animals, gradually became an ethical education, a systematic assault with months of testing to teach young males obedience, responsibility and the sacredness of the tribe. Reason, directed by an innate purpose, became responsible for social harmony, and aggression was channelled into a concern for social order through a spiritual activity. These too have been nearly abandoned today, as have families.

The second great event came with cortex enlargement, resulting from increasing demands of society, families and education: needs waiting for effectuating DNA modifications. Biological needs had long provoked innate commands subconsciously, but reasoned responses must be guided by what is known and nearly all known knowledge was innate. A wasp can construct a mud cocoon from an innate design, including innate standards for location, mud, and larvae. But reason must judge this-location-not-that according to the innate standards in the real world -- also for mud and larvae.

Cortex enlargement led to the opening up of a consciousness into which phylogenetic commands could enter, heralded as "feelings". Thus conscious reason began to share behavioral guidance with the genome, by cancelling or amplifying the responses. Thus fear can be checked by reason. Most revolutionary of all, really the core of the second event, reason's imagination became empowered to promulgate its own commands, apart from and even in violation of nature. Man could imagine things in support of natural law and his developing concept of humanness as genius, but he could also imagine violations of natural law and humanness; original sin is a stark reality producing the evil side to naturally good man -- as good as any animal. Rousseau taught that human beings were essentially good and equal in nature, and that it was civilization and property that corrupted them. Clearly it was not civilization but reason's imagination that created inhumanness; humanly purposed reason created the good, evilly-purposed reason the bad.

But natural law demands, in addition to a will to survive, an urge to rise up. Cortex expansion led to the opening up of a consciousness, with conscious reason, and a conscious memory which accumulated knowledge gained from reasoned experiences, enormously increasing the knowledge available to reason for producing rational responses. Consciousness opened up a fascinating world of conscious "feelings" (innate feelings, not mere temper or imagination): as an urge to belong to a communion, obey conscience, and deepest of all an often semi-conscious urge to rise up; "to know", and "to admire, the very taproot of civilization". This new inner or spiritual world would become central to culture.

Primitive men became consciously aware of innate social guidance, as "commands, kindred yet coming from the outside". Fascinated by the power and protectiveness of their clan, they came to see many new ideas modeled in it: hierarchy, order, and classes, of times of festivals, of space. They became aware of contradictions and so of wrong and of right, and of rationality as a conformability to a purpose. They became aware of *ideas* as such, and of the categories of class, time, space and so on, of Aristotle and Kant, so Durkheim concluded.(4)

All of this had to be discussed. The primitive language of gestures and sounds was adequate as a supplement for habit and tradition, but a more detailed encoding was required for the new abstract "ideas". Exhilaration, perhaps, strained sounds and gestures into verbs, and nouns followed, and so a syntactic encoding, again as a reasoned response to an inner urge.

Reflecting on their deep feelings of belonging to their society, with its protection, spiritual strength and mystic bonds, they felt a great "force" of preciousness which became the Great Spirit of the tribe. (The character of a people is in what they love, wrote St. Augustine.) God was Society and Society was God, their commands being identical. Revelations are claimed to come from God; our society we know did, or from Nature. The difference is only in the accommodations.

From social preciousness they conceived the categories of sacred and profane and developed "a system of ideas of how to represent to themselves the society of which they were members, and the intimate relations they had with it". "From the moment when men (became aware) of internal (invisible) connections between things (cause and effects), science and philosophy" and religion were born, wrote Durkheim. These had to be discussed, comprehended and celebrated; men were driven by an urge to represent all which came to them from their society and so evolved the first significant symbol, the first written word, their totem, "us". Durkheim deduced from a plethora of evidence that all major religions began as totemisms, with "religion", philosophy and science all as one: "the way things really are."

And so we come to the third great turning in the history of humanness. Culture, as knowledge from reasoned experiences which is passed on to offspring, began far back in the history of imitative learning. Young rats are known to learn by immitation to avoid certain poisons, corvids about certain predators, and primates numerous things, all of the physical world. The production of artifacts, first as design of tools, within the last half million year, gives evidence of the beginning of man's world of conscious reason. Paleolithic cave art of 35,000 to 12,000 years ago evidences a reaching for something beyond, as in "The Wild Horse of Montespan"; the art critic Fauré expressed it for Constable's landscapes as "I am the Resurrection and the Life".

Primitive man was not Hobbesian: poor, nasty and brutish; he was, in a moderate environment, free, exuberant and searching. We see him in the Paleolithic society that appreciated true art, and in the South Sea Islanders of Melville and Dana. Trilling quoted Schiller on the innocence of this state of harmony with nature as "A state . . . not merely met with before the dawn of civilization, but as also the state to which civilization aspires." The same spirituality exists in Greek art, as making the invisible visible; theirs was a spiritual religion of artists, poets and philosophers. "There is a life which is higher . . . men will live it . . . by virtue of something in them that is divine . . . small though it be, in power and worth it is far above the rest", wrote the unspiritual Aristotle.

Art is a sensitive indicator of spiritual feelings of humanness, or their absence. Van Doren Stern wrote of the Paleolithic maidens of LaMadelaine as "portraying the human form thousands of years in advance" of the 10,000 year later god-king art.(5) Leakey noted in Paleolithic art, techniques of perspective and movement "reinvented (only) with the Renaissance."(6) These were efforts to comprehend humanness as a spirituality beyond totemism. Recent studies have found the most and the best Paleolithic art to be located in cave chambers of greatest resonance, suggesting a chanting celebration.

Reasoned advances allowed the Paleolithic people to push back from the edge of subsistence, and when agriculture became intensive in great river valleys, some 10,000 years ago, the purpose of survival faded in the affluence as a source of tribal authority. In the disorder intellectuals may have grabbed a monopoly on knowledge and terrorized the masses into a sub-human servitude with threats of "angry gods". These god-king, priestly bureaucracies were neither proper civilizations nor religions; these first Statisms whose only purpose was power originated mass slavery, the teaching of superstitions as "angry gods" for social control, voluptuous courts, vestal virgins, and the evils of "religion" and tyranny. Religion as man's need for a spiritual life is innate; churches are his often erring responses, subject to reason's good and evil. Even Solomon's court had his thousand wives. Innovations were strongly proscribed for fear they might get out of control, early Lysenkoism. Plato remarked on the frozen nature of Egyptian art.

A hiatus in humanness as evidenced in art lasted for some 8000 years and was far deeper than the so-called Dark Ages. It might still exist today had it not been for human societies, such as the Greeks, beyond the easy reach of god-king tyrannies. Modern Statists recognize that their control must be global as did Marx and Lenin, for sub-human servitude cannot be maintained in sight of free men.

Rationality requires a conformability to an overall purpose, like the parts of a smoothly running machine. Rationality, purpose and truth constitute a little recognized unity; one cannot be had without all three. Life had been held rational for a billion years by the overarching purposes of survival and rising up. With the affluence of agriculture, suddenly it was gone, except in the remaining tribal societies around the world.

Progress was very slow in the god-king empires, considering the time and facilities available. There was a collecting of knowledge and some progress, and the Greek became fascinated with their learning, but they also came to fear the priesthoods, "Seers who bring terror to keep men afraid" (Aeschylus). It may have been this fear that urged their intuitive adoption of a guiding purpose, to keep them from the seen abyss. In any case by focusing their social efforts with a purpose, to seek that "proper to man", they created a supreme culture which evolved the spirit and became the foundation of Western civilization. This socially imposed purpose, explicated in a culture, constitutes humanity's third great turning. Culture was to be something entirely new: an explication and celebration of an overarching rationalizing social purpose, to seek a humanness, a rising up, through a socially imposed purpose as a replacement for the primitive, externally imposed, unmanipulatable purpose of survival. From the beginning of man's conscious struggle to rise up, it was against his external environment, a physical world, that he strove; in the future it would increasingly be a contest within himself and his society, as a spiritual domain, of feelings and imagination, for comprehending and following a human purpose for social guidance, and still in the end for survival.

Progress was far greater in 800 years of Greece than in 8000 of the so-called "civilizations" of god-king empires. The Greeks lost their purpose, never recognizing its implacable essentiality, *nor is it recognized today.* Christianity took the equivalent purpose, proper to God, and similar progress was made in the years of the Christian world following the fall of Rome. Central to culture must be a purpose which guides social rationality, as conformable to traditions of a sacred past expressed in special symbols and reinforced with festivals in which all participate.

This was done by the priesthoods of the god-king empires, but only in celebration of the ruling power. The great innovation of the Christian world was the creation of a "church", in which all members became believing supporters. Church organizations worked with the common people, guiding and helping them in their lives. This created a vast new organization, the essential purpose of which was maintaining adherence to their human purpose, participated in by all. Social motivation which must be taught and upheld, becomes eviscerated when an intellectual clique undermines it. Machiavelli spelled it out; he advised his intellectual colleagues to cease urging the restraint essential for social order on the commons; promise them their fondest dreams and they will follow us as gods.

The Reasoners abandoned religion as superstition and thereby discarded purpose; it could have been changed back to "proper to man". That the shift to the loose-cannon of un-purposed reason was intentional is evident in their acquiescence to de Sade's rollicking deduction that without purpose nothing can be forbidden, and in the Enlightenment's loosening of the bonds of human society for an "individualism". Meanwhile "The Economists" began (1755) generating the essentials of collectivist ideology as a replacement for the culture of a self governing human society. There was to be no property, religion or families; everything was to be in the State, with absolute equality, except of course for the bureaucracy, and "at age five children taken from their parents . . . " (See *Morelly's Code* in Tocqueville's *Ancient Regime)*(7), -- a century before Marx, and two and a half centuries before the "reforms" of today's intellectuals.

But people object that modernism does show progress; look around at such wonders. Yes progress has continued in our physical world, because science has, in the past at least, clung resolutely to the guiding purpose of seeking truth, where there is and must be a right and wrong. Eminent scholars, discussing C.P. Snow's confounding *Two Cultures'* suggestion of "supplanting" culture with science(8), declared science "stands like Gibraltar".(9) The humanities have become just another "peep show" in a dark world of relativism, drained of purpose to stand on. They need to "stand like the Sun!", lighting man's society and soul, even Gibraltar.

For science cannot "serve the instinct for conduct and beauty" so essential for humanness, declared Matthew Arnold in his debate of 1882 with T.H. Huxley.(10) However, when ideology replaces culture, as Hegel perceived, imagination and theory replace purpose for guidance. Humanness and human culture must rest on knowledge acquired from reasoned experiences about that proper to man, not on ethereal theories. Mill, again, declared that the base for the Western canon was nowhere to be found more lucidly than in the classical literature of the Greeks. Their sculpture and literature, barely approached since, and the great art, music and drama of pre-modernity were a guide to and a celebration of humanness.

The modern attack on Western culture (civilization) is intended to destroy not only the Western or "white man's" culture but to replace *the very concept of culture as social guidance with ideology.* Western culture was never just Western, nor all "white"; it included the best from around the world: Semitic, Hindu, and Chinese. For irascible individuals to live together peacefully, cooperatively, and productively requires an imposition of rules for social order: the non-aggression and altruism of natural law. These must be taught, as an explication, exemplification and celebration of the purpose: to be human, with a spiritual life, standards, decency and a responsibility to support these in a self government. Statists recognize that these conflict with "overhead planning", hence culture as social guidance must be terminated, transformed to mere entertainment: sports, infantility and the erotic, adequate for sub-humanness.

Not confrontation and zealotry but a quiet and felicitous outspreading of truth is the need of supporters of human society in their struggle against Statism. Truth and a unity of effort must be carried from person to person, from group to group until a complete network for communication and discussion is achieved. Seek truth for all, but join in confidence only with those found to be trustworthy. Confrontation and loud talk will bring swift reprisal from Statists. Who can object to truth and humanness? For those who murmur, do as Paul ordered "Have nothing to do with them that they might feel ashamed"; but be open to them, that they might come over.(11)

Surely there is nothing here which has not been long known, and warned of by our Founders, Tocqueville, Nietzsche, Nobelist Albert Schweitzer, and spelled out in detail in 1936 by Walter Lippmann. Barbara Ward, British Labor Party "spokesman" and scholar, wrote in 1951 of "the Western experiment, the most audacious and exhilarating of mankind . . . appears to be on the defensive . . . The world of freedom closes. The Western vision fades . . . glimpses of Moloch and Baal the terrible gods of the State reasserting their ancient sway."(12)

Imagine a world where "Language (as literature and writing) no longer exists"; a world denuded of the human preciousness of family, love, modesty and honor; a world in which "social policy relying on private responsibility" has been abandoned. All of these have been proclaimed by "professors", and thus the freedom of self-government which people have struggled over two dozen centuries to grasp is relinquished with indifferences. John Adams warned us that "Democracy . . . wastes, exhausts, and murders itself. There never was a democracy that did not commit suicide," because democracy and equality are both poison to human society.

For initial action, don't demand the truth, find it out! About everything of our evil century, especially about WW II and Vietnam, Rodney King and Waco, and about our corrupted education, rule of law, families, and the unopposed social deracination by a media-academia complex. People who can see the reality of the darkness descending must help in a revival of human society.

PART TWO   INTRODUCTION

Part One presented the physical and historical evidence of our forebears rising up monotonically for seven million years, and creating culture, religion, a syntactic language, self-government, and the humanness to produce the miraculous art of European Paleolithic caves. They were driven by an imposed purpose, but around 10,000 years ago they were carried beyond their purpose, and their guidance and rationality were lost.

No more solid evidence exists, for the need for an organized society with leadership for self-government under such a purpose, than when social purpose was lost 10,000 years ago, order was regained only by the terror of totalitarianism. Intellectuals had no experience, no history, to guide them out of the irrationality of lost purpose following the agricultural revolution; there was little other than terror available to regain social order, and they presented themselves as gods. The Greeks, on barren land still struggling for survival, had never lost their organized society, and were able to impose upon themselves a new and more effective purpose in raising up. And the Christians, either by intuition or obvious need, created a new and universal organization a church to teach and to lead in supporting a human purpose.

The greatness of post-Renaissance society, and a decay in Christian motivation, apparently fired the greed of intellectuals for again grasping for total power. We are told that after Lenin succeeded, he searched Marx diligently for what to do now, and found nothing. Again, only "terror without end" would serve. But again, tyranny fell; it cannot survive in sight of free men. Hence today's intellectuals seek a global hegemony.

Part Two presents the consequences of four centuries of undermining of essential social institutions, leading to the final onslaught of collectivists, and WW II. The importance here lies in that the evidence for the contrivance of WW II by Franklin Roosevelt is so solid, so complete and interlocking, that when people reflect on the horror of what he effected, and in the mainstream's covering up, even to today, it opens minds to what followed. The true horror is not so much the renegadism itself, but that it has all been so dissembled by so many people for so long.

WW II would have been impossible without the solid support of the new collectivist Establishment of "overhead planners"; "no other approach even considered" declared astute social observer, Walter Lippmann, in 1936. This support had been prepared by "going through the institutions", transforming them from supporting pillars of human society, into agencies of Statism: John Dewey in education, Morris Cohen in Constitutional rule of law. Franz Boas and many others began an attack on Western civilization.

Following their great success in WW II, intellectuals turned to complete their subversion of social institutions by conspiracy, and finally by stepping forward and openly presenting their intentions to replace self government and Western civilization with their rule.

VI WORLD WAR II

WW II was like a vast cyclone that swept everything into its maw, even as it continued to spin off new destruction, changing and degrading the world into a far more inhuman place with little honor or decency. The acclaimed liberal Arthur Schlesinger Jr. admitted in 1948, after three Pearl Harbor Reports were released by the government (1945-46), that Franklin Roosevelt had "tricked" America into the war.(1) That is, he baited the Japanese into attacking, thus gaining entrance to the Soviet-German War.

Then in 1990, Mr. Schlesinger told us *why* FDR had so brutally sacrificed thousands of young lives at Pearl Harbor and thousands more on Bataan, nearly destroying Western civilization in a terrible horror the likes of which the world had never seen. Mr. Roosevelt had a "vision", you see. He wanted to "narrow the differences" between Communism and democracy, by America becoming nearly half pregnant with Communism.(2) We all know what that means.

Should you doubt his explanation, note that it is the actual result of WW II, as Mr. Schlesinger went on to insist rather admiringly; look at the record. Also in his "day of infamy" speech, dictated at 5PM according to his secretary Grace Tully(3), we are told twice that Hawaii and Manila were bombed simultaneously; actually Manila would not be bombed for another six hours. This suggests the possibility that neither had been bombed when the draft was first written as supported by other facts.(3A) To advance his trickery, he sent out an executive order to all defense plants and involved government agencies giving top priority to Stalin on all supplies, ahead even of our own men fighting the desperate war in the Pacific into which he had flung them.

A few months later, in Casablanca, his son Elliott has informed us, he came up with the idea of "unconditional surrender" while "thoughtfully sucking a tooth". "Just the thing . . . Uncle Joe might have made it up himself".(4) It was recognized by everyone who would look that unconditional surrender would leave no basis for ending the disaster short of total destruction, with Communism taking all. Secretary of State Hull declared in his Memoirs that Churchill was "dumbfounded". Adm. Leahy, Roosevelt's very reserved Chief of Staff, branded it "unwise". Maj. Gen. Fuller declared the war would take on "the horrors of a war of religion", in the end the Soviets "would dominate Europe".(5)

Had Roosevelt tricked Americans into the bloody war truly "for their own good", as Harry Truman was to assert, that could only have been to preserve Western civilization. "Joining Stalin to impose freedom was a travesty . . . a gargantuan jest", charged former President Hoover, who had been active in WW I. The claim to be "destroying Hitler" was a "deceit of indirection", the flip side of which was clearly the empowerment of Stalin and Communism by removal of their principal opposition.

In 1939, we were told in high school that we would have to go to war to end the idea that the State should have the power to dictate how people are to live and think. Yet the predominate result of WW II has been the very opposite, the empowerment of Statism around the world. Over 85 percent of the people were strongly America First in spirit, and wanted no part in another European war. Yet after Pearl Harbor nearly a million of us volunteered and many millions answered Franklin Roosevelt's "day of infamy" call. We did not then know, as we do now, that FDR had baited the Japanese into the attack against an unprepared Pearl Harbor.

This would have been impossible without the collectivist establishment developed by the network of socialist cells that had been formed in our major universities even as the century was beginning. "Every year the Communist Student League graduated its hundreds from the colleges". Then came "the years that floated Alger Hiss into the party and made possible the big underground, the infiltration of government, education, and all branches of communications, especially radio, motion pictures, books, magazine and newspaper publishing". "They came not singly but in clusters . . . knowing and influencing one another . . . A small intellectual army passed over to the Communist Party"; Whittaker Chambers so wrote and he was there.(6) By 1936 the astute observer, Walter Lippmann, had perceived that Chambers' "intellectual army" had made "overhead planning", of collectivists, the prevailing dogma. "Only a handful here and there, groups without influence . . . continue to challenge it." Without the knowledge of their presence and support, Franklin Roosevelt would never have dared to bait the Japanese into an attack and then under cover of wartime security, ally himself with the evil Stalinist regime that was then acknowledged to be the greatest danger to Western civilization. (See Chap. IV, Ref. 7)

The plan to sacrifice, deliberately and evilly, the lives of thousands of young men at Pearl Harbor and on Bataan to provide FDR entry into the Soviet-German War, like sacrificing pawns for board position, was only the beginning of the treachery. Roosevelt had made his intentions clear on January 10, 1941, note the date as nearly a year before Pearl Harbor; Harry Hopkins was sent to meet Churchill with FDR's "cause", even as Stalin and Hitler were allies, carving up old Europe from Finland to France. It was "to be the defeat, ruin and slaughter of Hitler, *to the exclusion of all other purposes, loyalties, or aims*" (e.a.). Gen. A.C. Wedemeyer, the most scholarly of WW II generals, wrote "thus the President of the United States renounced adherence to the Constitution and dishonored his pledge to the American people to keep them out of a foreign war . . . ".(7)

Why was his "cause" not his "Four Freedoms" that he was to seek to dupe the American public into believing? Why not the defeat of all totalitarianism? Stalinism was universally recognized as the greatest danger to America and Western civilization. Why not slaughter both? Or after July, 1941, let them slaughter each other? Maj. Gen, J.F.C. Fuller declared that "annihilation (unconditional surrender) bereft the Western allies' cause of a sane war aim".(8)

More significantly, why not take advantage of powerful German Army forces that, according to reliable reports would, with a show of outside support, themselves slaughter Hitler and the Nazi Party? This could have created a Europe united against totalitarianism, saved Western civilization mortal damage, and brought an early end to the enslavement and murder of millions. Only recently publicized is the fact that British Foreign Office papers present Pope Pius XII offering, early on (1940), to risk the papacy as mediator between German generals and British negotiators for overthrow of the Nazi Party.(9) Slaughtering only Hitler was a deceit of indirection; destroying Germany meant bringing Communism into Europe. Empowering Stalin meant bringing Communism to Asia and America. "I give him everything I can and ask nothing in return," FDR told his friend, George Bullitt.(10) To sacrifice thousands of human lives, for other than the protection of home and human society, is a supreme crime. Had Franklin Roosevelt believed it necessary, and had acted to save Western civilization and the lives of endangered millions, he could be forgiven. However, that was not his purpose.

There is no clearer proof of Franklin Roosevelt's perfidy and equivalence with the dictators, than his refusal even to investigate these increasingly urgent feelers, coming through Switzerland from groups within Germany, from Army high command and from civilian leaders, wishing to overthrow the Nazi regime. These became even more insistent after the Germans were thrown back from Moscow, actually before Pearl Harbor. An even greater evil was the media's supportive silence and the entire intellectual-liberal regime's acquiescence. Certainly one of the greatest crimes of WW II was this exclusion of the greatest nation of Europe from the anti-totalitarian forces, while welcoming the other war aggressor, that later refused that opportunity.

The historical trail of Franklin Roosevelt's intent begins with his first major foreign policy move; within months of his inauguration in 1933 he gave U.S. recognition to the Soviet regime, even as the bodies of millions of Stalin's starved peasants stunk on the plains of the Ukraine. In 1936, he appointed "the corrupt and gullible Joseph Davies" as Ambassador to the Soviet with instructions "to win Stalin's friendship at all costs".(11) Within five months "the superbly informed embassy staff, backed by a highly professional division of Eastern Europeans affairs in the State Department . . . (with) better records on Soviet policy then the Soviet government itself", was abolished, dispersed, and destroyed.(12)

In the Thirties intellectuals, along with the leaders in Hollywood and New York, were predominantly Communist partisans. When a small group of liberal ex-Communists and Trotskyists published a "manifesto" in the Spring of 1939, denouncing the "totalitarian idea enthroned in Germany and Russia, . . . (with) thousands (in both) imprisoned or tortured . . . ", the renegade, intellectual establishment described by Lippmann rose up in wrath. In an "Open Letter" signed by "400" Soviet supporters, the manifestoites were vilified as "fascists", Trotskyists, and it was a "fantastic falsehood that Russia had anything in common with Germany." Hypocrisy was the mark of the whole century; "red baiting" as criticizing Communists was as reprehensible as anti-Semitism in criticizing Jews. Most unhappily, the very issue of *The Nation* in which the 400's "Letter" appeared carried also a last-minute spot announcement of the Stalin-Hitler Pact (Aug. 1939). From then on the "400" and the similarly minded became the major supporters, the "isolationist activists", for "peace" and against American "imperialism". These incidents are described fully by a manifesto participant, Eugene Lyons.(13)

Information was placed in Franklin Roosevelt's hands in the fall of 1940 that a machine, to be called "Magic", had been perfected by W.F. Friedman that could routinely decode intercepts of the "unbreakable" Japanese Purple Code.(14) Then late in the 1940 campaign for a third term he orated, "I shall say it again, and again, and agaaain: Your boys are not going to be sent into a foreign war". Hardly a dozen weeks later he sent his "Cause message to Churchill", by Harry Hopkins in January, 1941; and it was widely recognized that by "slaughtering Hitler", the doorway to Europe would be opened for Stalin.

But first, dragging America into a war in which the totalitarian states, the Soviet and Germany, were allies waging a war of aggression from France to Finland, which more than 85 percent of Americans were vehemently against, would require what Arthur Schlesinger was later to term "trickery".(15) While he was at it he scolded the liberal historian, C.A. Beard, for laying out FDR's trickery, "like a prosecuting attorney".(16) George Morgenstern's *Pearl Harbor*(17) has another excellent account of the pre-war maneuvering and George Crocker's *Roosevelt's Road to Russia*(18) continues with a very concise account of the diplomacy of the war years, through Yalta.

Three major investigations of the Pearl Harbor incident produced three principal official reports, of "The Army Pearl Harbor Board", a "Navy Court of Inquiry"(19), and of a "Joint Congressional Committee"(20). Crocker's book contains an excellent compilation of diaries and memoirs of important wartime figures, and some of these should be read by anyone who desires the real truth about WW II and Franklin Roosevelt. Only a few incidents will be examined here, to reveal Roosevelt's unmistakable intentions. The intent here is not to belittle historical figures but to provide an account of the history that people need to comprehend as to how the horrors of the past century came about.

Admiral J.O. Richardson was made commander of the United States Fleet and of the Pacific Fleet in January, 1940, and was soon maneuvered into changing the stationing of the fleet from the West Coast to Pearl Harbor. Richardson became aware of the deficiencies in the defensive and offensive capabilities of the fleet and of the base, and began to argue for a return of the fleet to the mainland to be "docked, manned, stocked and stripped" for war, in light of the increasingly unsettled conditions. In October, 1940, he was received by Roosevelt, and tried to impress upon the president the danger in leaving an unprepared fleet exposed at Pearl Harbor, and the need for preparations for wartime service. Richardson was abruptly removed from his command in the middle of his term, in February, 1941. On requesting a reason he was told he "had hurt the President's feelings".(21)

In the two critical years of the Stalin-Hitler pact, August, 1939 to June, 1941, two groups with very opposite intentions urged American isolation from the conflict being waged in Europe between the "democracies", Britain principally and France, and the totalitarian regimes of the Soviets and Germany. These were the America Firsters who despised and feared both totalitarian powers, while urging arming for preparedness. The other group is never discussed or described; basically they were the liberals, leftists, socialists and communists who sought to prevent our arming against the Stalin-Hitler Pact countries. Labor leaders and others who denied being Communists but later were found to be were active in strikes, work stoppages, and violence, to cripple defense production, often deceitfully blamed on America Firsters.(22)

When Germany attacked the Soviets in June, 1941, beating Stalin to the punch, Franklin Roosevelt went to work in earnest. He ordered the Navy to determine "what the Japs would do" if he put an embargo on oil to them (British and Dutch companies already had). When told that Japan would be forced into war "to go get some", he was also advised by the Navy not to embargo oil to them because it would precipitate war. Ignoring the advice he issued an executive order virtually embargoing all trade with Japan, closed the Panama Canal to Japanese shipping, and froze all Japanese assets.(23)

A more moderate Japanese government came to power and Premier Prince Konoye began seeking a conference with Roosevelt, as the economic sanctions were grinding the Japanese economy and society to a quick halt. Roosevelt complained of the time required for a Hawaiian meeting; how about Juneau, Alaska? The Japanese accepted and suggested September 21 to 25. Then Roosevelt began backing off. American Ambassador Grew, a nine-year expert on Japan, pleaded with Roosevelt to accept. In his diary he wrote, "For a prime minister of Japan to shatter all precedents . . . and come hat-in-hand to meet the President . . . on American soil is a gauge of his determination" to maintain peace.(24)

The Japanese economy had been quickly reduced "to a desperate pass"; Oct. 15 slipped by, the final date for a conference. The Konoye cabinet resigned; the militarists took over and on Nov. 20-21 Japan offered a last ditch *modus vivendi*, which Hull would describe as a "final proposition". His answer sent on Nov. 26 was described as an "ultimatum".(25) It was clearly never intended to be acceptable; Churchill had a hand in toughening it up. The Army Board described it as "touching the button that started the war". At a War Cabinet meeting, FDR stated that "we are likely to be attacked, as soon as Monday, Dec. 1".(26)

During the entire year of 1941, and beyond, FDR and Marshall knew ahead of time what the Japanese were planning through "Magic intercepts" of top secret messages. They received the secret messages concerning all negotiations between Tokyo and their Ambassador Nomura as soon as he did: the "wind" alert and the "pilot" message, nearly everything. On Nov. 19 a Magic intercept informed Washington of the special "winds" message, which was to be encoded in the regular Japanese overseas radio broadcast from Station J-A-P in Tokyo; it would inform all nationals when war should become imminent. In early afternoon of Dec. 4 it was learned that the Japanese Navy had changed its code, and orders were sent to Japanese embassies to destroy their codes. Several hours later, the "winds" execute message was received, so the Army Pearl Harbor Board reported and as testified before the Joint Congressional Committee.

It is necessary to inject here a parallel course of events before returning to "winds". The number and activity of Japanese spies had been increasing, particularly on Oahu, as was FBI monitoring. However, Roosevelt never interfered with spying activities, which is most important to recall later in connection with the so-called "Jap internment". The FBI was monitoring both the messages which the spies received and those sent out to Tokyo. As the autumn of 1941 moved into late November, the reporting of all ship positions at Pearl Harbor was increased in frequency and in preciseness as to "double bunking", and so on.(27) These reports left no doubt as to the aim of a Japanese attack. For Roosevelt to have had these spies arrested would have blinded the Japanese war planners, and thereby have probably prevented the attack -- something that Franklin Roosevelt above all did not want. These spy cases, some 3000, were never publicized for two reasons: the top secrecy of Magic would be compromised, but more urgent was the necessity for FDR to avoid having to explain why the spies had not been interfered with for over a year. Thus arose the perception of "loyal Japanese"(27A).

Receipt of "winds" sparked at least three officers into attempting to force through warnings to Pearl Harbor. Navy Captain McCollum met with a number of high officers, including Adm. Stark, Chief of Naval Operations and Adms. Turner and Ingersoll to that end, but the message he had prepared was never sent.(28) Army Colonels D.K. Sadtler and R.S. Bratton also tried to warn Pearl Harbor. Col. Sadtler went to Gen. Gerow, Chief of War Plans, and to a Col. W.B. Smith, secretary to the general staff, but all warnings were rejected(29).

Those who would deny the deceptions that resulted in Pearl Harbor insist that the Pearl Commanders had been sent a "War Warning". In every lie there must be some grain of truth. A "Warning" was sent, but it was a Class C warning, calling only for a "sabotage alert". This warning led to ammunition being stored and airplanes bunched, *as immediately reported to Washington.* No correction was received. Note this was the very opposite to that required for an attack, but ideal for a Pearl Harbor. The Army Board dismissed the "war warning"; "had a full war message been sent, Hawaii could have been ready."(30)

But again, as in the case of the "winds" message, that is exactly what FDR did not want; a "Pearl Harbor" was needed. He knew by Dec. 5 that the Japanese Task Force (which was steaming toward Hawaii through the North Pacific from which Roosevelt had thoughtfully ordered all American ships and planes) had strict orders to turn away if it was found that surprise had been lost; again, that Roosevelt did not want. Franklin Roosevelt had allowed a Magic machine to be sent to the Canal Zone and another to Churchill, but Hawaii was not allowed to know even of their existence. Nor were the Pearl Commanders given any information collected from Japanese spies (or even their existence) by the FBI operating in their midst.

The last Japanese message was to arrive in two sections; the first "pilot" message, at about 11:00 a.m. on Dec. 6, was an answer to Hull's hard "ultimatum" of Nov. 27 and was likewise a hard rejection of Hull's message. The final section, expected to give the time of hostilities, would come later. These were Purple coded messages, not to Washington, but to their Ambassador who was to deliver an appropriate response. They were intercepted, decoded by Magic, and the first section was translated and delivered by 9PM, Dec. 6. A Commander Schulz delivered the first section, of thirteen parts, to FDR about 9:30PM. Roosevelt read it, Schulz testified to the Joint Committee, handed it to Hopkins and exclaimed 'This means war!"(31)

The final section, delivered by Capt. Kramer to Adm. Stark at 9AM, Dec. 7, setting 1PM (7AM, sunrise over Oahu) as time for the attack. It was testified he cried out, "My God . . . I must get word to Kimmel at once".(32) But he didn't. Gen. Marshall's copy was delivered to his staff secretary Col. W.B. Smith, who made no attempt to deliver the message. Kramer attempted to find Marshall; Col. Bratton, Chief for Eastern G-2, also went looking for Marshall.(33)

In the Report of the Joint Committee is the testimony

of Representative Keefe: "Gen. Marshall . . . had the 'pilot' message . . . on the afternoon of Dec. 6 . . . placing on him an obligation to . . . receive the subsequent information (section two) . . . soon forthcoming. He did not do so. The alleged failure of . . . (Col. Smith, secretary to his General Staff) to furnish (him) promptly with (the final section) was unusual . . . (and) Gen. Marshall made no effort to ascertain why such a colossal breakdown should occur . . . on the eve of war".(34) What constitutes treason?

But Marshall, on what he knew was the most important day in his life, had gone on a long morning canter. He wandered into his office at 11:25AM. He could have reached the Pearl Commanders in ten minutes by a special scrambler phone. In the nearly two hours remaining before the attack, Pearl Harbor could have launched at least a token flight of airplanes and readied guns. But Marshall and FDR knew that that would very likely cause the Jap fleet to turn away, as ordered on losing the advantage of surprise. So he didn't. He fooled around getting a message for Gen. Short dispatched at 12:18PM(35), one hour and seven minutes before first bombs. It carried no "priority", was not marked "urgent", and Marshall had it sent by "RCA commercial wire".(36) A boy was pedalling it through the streets of Honolulu when the bombs started falling. "When treason prospers none dare call it treason."

Sunday morning, Dec. 7, 1941, Franklin Roosevelt had his "stamp collection" out, while Harry Hopkins lounged about and photographers were available. Adm. Beardsall delivered to FDR's bedroom the final section at 10AM(37), three hours before the attack. He had 23 hours in which to prepare his "day of infamy" speech, and to get his dander up for a proper display of enragement.

Colonels Sadtler and Bratton who tried faithfully to execute their proper duties, along with Navy Captains Safford and McCollum, remained in minor posts, unpromoted.(38) On the other hand Colonel Smith who failed even to try to deliver the final message to Marshall, was shortly a three star Lt.

General Walter Bedell Smith(39), given the honor of receiving the German surrender, and much else. The Magic genius W.F. Friedman principal cryptanalyst for the War Dept, (who is said to have exclaimed when he heard the news of Pearl Harbor, "They knew! They knew!") told Captain Safford that Col. Bissell had "destroyed all copies of the winds message, by order of General Marshall"(40); Bissell was soon a Brig. General. Captain Safford was the Chief radio intelligence officer of Naval communications, and was in a position to, and did, give the most damning evidence concerning "winds". Neither Bissell nor Friedman were asked (allowed) to testify by the majority party.

Adm. King who blamed "the people" for Pearl Harbor, as did Harry Truman and Arthur Schlesinger, was made one of the first five star admirals. Adm. Stark though reprimanded by the Joint Committee for "failure to perform responsibilities" was assigned Commander U.S. Naval Forces in Europe and awarded a second Distinguished Service Medal by Roosevelt. Gen. Gerow, castigated in all three Pearl Harbor reports, was promoted and given command of the 15th Army in Europe and later appointed Commandant of the General Staff School at Fort Leavenworth. Hull who buried the world in a catastrophic war was given the Nobel "Peace Prize", and Marshall became Secretary of State.

Marshall is unique among world leaders; he never did nor did he allow anyone else to write his story. He graduated from VMI and soon entered the Army as a second lieutenant. He served in WW I, apparently credibly, for he reached a position on General Pershing's staff. Reverting to a peacetime captain he suffered the boredom and disappointment of the peacetime Army.

As a lieutenant colonel in 1933 he asked Gen. Pershing to intercede with Chief of Staff Douglas MacArthur. Marshall's record showed insufficient time commanding troops so MacArthur gave him command of the Eighth Regiment with an advance to colonel. In one year his regiment dropped from one of the best to one of the worst. He failed to be promoted to general; the Inspector General declared him "incompetent to handle troops."

Pushed from the line of promotion, Marshall wandered into the National Guard, and then to the Civil Conservation Corp of young men planting trees, building small anti-erosion dams and other conservation measures. Mrs. Marshall in her book *Together* tells of his openings of new camps as gala affairs. One of his camps was rated the best in the Corp; it was through such activities that he attracted the attention of Mrs. Roosevelt and Harry Hopkins, who recognized in his modest abilities their man, who would do what he was told. By 1936 he was a brigadier with a command, in 1938 Assistant Chief of Staff, becoming in 1939 Chief of Staff --pushed ahead of 34 other generals.

While Chief of Staff during the war years, there is evidence from an investigation by the House Special Committee on Military Affairs that known Communists were given commissions. There was also a famous attempted destruction of files on subversives, which must have involved the highest authority, and was frustrated only by the persistence of Senator Bridges from New Hampshire.

During the war Marshall was found to be favoring the same policies that Stalin urged America to follow: a second front, and no Balkan invasion. He turned down both a request from Hull's State Department and a separate one from the British, for a secure corridor into Berlin.

At Teheran Roosevelt agreed to pushing Poland westward, so that Stalin could move his boundary. This led to the eventual holocausting of over ten million people from homes held as long as London was English. Largely women and children were pushed onto the open road with what they could carry on their backs. Only freezing rain and snow brought relief from marauding Soviet troops, robbing, raping, murdering. Roosevelt's diplomat, Geo. F. Kennan, wrote in his *Memoirs*,(41) in "considerable sections of Eastern Europe scarcely a man, woman, or child was left alive".

Perhaps some 600,000 of these pitiful refugees had doubled the size of Dresden, so at Yalta Roosevelt agreed to an annihilation bombing of Dresden, to remove back pressure on Stalin's ethnic cleansing; there was no military objective. Bombing was done in three vast waves, spaced so as to catch relief crews out. An enormous "firestorm engulfed eight square miles". "Not enough survivors were left to bury the dead. Troops moved in and collected piles of corpses. Steel grills 25 feet across were constructed to be fueled with wood and straw, and batches of 500 corpses were piled on. Funeral pyres were still burning a fortnight later". So wrote Paul Johnson in his *Modern Times*.(42)

After Yalta, Marshall was assigned to break the bad news to the head of the Polish fighting forces, General Anders, whose men had served in so many critical battles and now would never be able to go home. Release of the shameful communique was only hours away. Irritated and weary Marshall would only say, "We continue to march with the Soviets . . . afterwards God alone knows".(43) If he was beginning to become aware of the enormity of the crime in which he had participated, his subsequent efforts, particularly in regard to China, do not show it.

General MacArthur and Admiral Nimitz had told Franklin Roosevelt at Pearl Harbor, in the presence of the President's Chief of Staff Admiral Leahy, that "Japan . . . (would) surrender by the use of sea and air power" without an invasion. Soon afterwards, in October, much of the remainder of the Japanese Fleet was crushed at Leyte, and Japan was bombed continuously from the Marianas.

When Roosevelt went to Yalta (Feb., 1945), he agreed that territory belonging to Japan and China would be transferred to the Soviet Union as inducements for Stalin to enter the uncalled for invasion of Japan; MacArthur and Nimitz were kept far away and uninformed. In the meantime, Roosevelt had created in the states a vast invasion force that was stopped only by the success of the atom bombs.

Roosevelt-Truman would have sacrificed perhaps two million people in an invasion carried out apparently for the sole purpose of giving Stalin a stake in the peace.

Roosevelt knew that the Yalta agreements, had no chance of passage in the Senate, as a peace treaty, hence arrogantly he merely proclaimed it "by me",(44) knowing that the media hovering in the wings would support him. FDR's lifelong friend and close political associate, Wm. Bullitt, wrote of Yalta, "No more unnecessary, disgraceful, and dangerous document has ever been signed by a president of the U.S."(45)

Roosevelt personally handed out to Stalin not only strategically important territories belonging to Japan and to China, he gave 100 shiploads of material; 860,410 tons dry cargo and 206,000 tons of liquid cargo, which included 75,000 trucks, 3,000 tanks, 5,000 airplanes. All for an un-needed invasion; actually it was to equip Stalin's 1,500,000 Far Eastern Army which would control Eastern Asia.

"While our armed forces were fighting with superb skill and courage", wrote Bullitt,(46) "our foreign policy was handled with reckless disregard of the vital interests of the American people". It was the interests of Stalin that came first, not the Jews and certainly not of the American people nor Western civilization.

The real evil however was not so much in Franklin Roosevelt, Harry Hopkins, and Eleanor, traitors there will always be, as it was in the hundreds of people who knew of his evil and did nothing, and especially in the media that was aware of the treason and shielded it from wider observation. Wm. Bullitt spoke but his warnings fell in a hollow chamber.

Elliott Roosevelt relates the sharp and continuing conflict between FDR's desire to promote Stalin and Churchill's "unceasing battle" to prevent Soviet post-war dominance in Europe.(47) Gen. J.R. Deane, in charge of Soviet Lend-Lease in Moscow, declared that Harry Hopkins carried out the Soviet aid program "with a zeal which approached fanaticism . . . that could not be tempered."(48) *Verona* showed conclusively . . . (that) working for Soviet Intelligence was Harry Hopkins".(49) "We knew who was giving information to the Soviets, and never prosecuted them . . . (nor) the cipher clerk who told the Soviets (about Verona). We did not prosecute anybody . . . details were suppressed . . . uncertainties fueled a culture war . . . ", Senator Daniel Patrick Moynihan.(50) General Groves testified concerning the struggle between the Manhattan (atomic) Project and Hopkins' Lend-Less Project.(51)

An entire chapter has been devoted to WW II for two major reasons. Never before in history has a government, or even a tyrannical regime, sacrificed so many lives to get into a war. Second, Franklin Roosevelt's brazen appropriation of government and social facilities and power, for purposes dangerously subversive to the nation, set an example followed by successive renegades. Thus, renegades in government and media joined in destroying the government of the small nation of Vietnam struggling against world Communism, when all major advisors warned that chaos would result. Later, concerning the trial of the Rodney King arresting officer, competent and impartial observers claimed no "miscarriage of justice", but liberal renegades in both government and media who had a week from trial's end to the announced acquittal did nothing to counter a threatened riot; then when the acquittal came, they actually incited a billion dollar looting of L.A. That Wm. and Hillary Clinton used the institutions of government, the FBI and Secret Service, IRS, Courts, Congress, and Cabinet, especially the Department of Justice, and the entire bureaucracy, as their personal vassals, for felonious and indecent ends was as much as admitted by Democratic Party seniors in their attempts to avoid impeachment.

NOTE ON WW II

This short chapter on WW II was never intended to do more than to present a minimum (but unquestionable) truth of the reality of the WW II treason. "America provoked Japan to such an extent the Japanese were forced to attack . . . (it) is a travesty of history ever to say that America was forced into war", Churchill's war production minister Lyttelton declared (6,20,44) to the American Chamber of Commerce. It is not just Franklin Roosevelt and his advisers, but the entire liberal establishment, particularly the *Times, Post,* and radio networks, and liberal political leaders who are responsible, for the appalling destruction of civilization, "The Holocaust", and the Cold War. It was Franklin Roosevelt's WW II and his alliance with Stalin's Communism that lead directly to corruption of our social institutions: families, rule of law, education and social coherence.

When that truth has been absorbed, along with how it has been repeatedly ignored or treated with indifference, on what basis can one object to Clinton, to Waco and Oklahoma, or object to corruption in education, media, jurisprudence, entertainment, and in our youth? Nor is their reason to doubt the treason that destroyed the South Viet government and abandoned the Viet victory that had been achieved, and then manufactured Watergate. No reason to object to abandoning human society and to submergence in a sub-human servitude to an evil regime.

VII WAR ON HUMAN SOCIETY

Nothing is more certain in the real world than power, the power of the organized and purposed, over the unorganized and directionless. Few things are as pitiful as a person who has lost all purpose in life, but the results are far more catastrophic when a whole society or civilization loses its purpose and its rationality. It is culture that must provide social guidance through purpose, and so the teaching and upholding of culture is a supremely important social function and the choice as a target of subversion by social renegades.

It was the Christian churches that guided and taught Western culture for much of two millennia. In early America it was the quality of the Calvinist schools that created the "flowering of New England" and produced most of America's famous authors, poets, and philosophers. Great developments and progress require work and discipline, however when accomplishments mount there are always those who will scheme, no longer to progress, but to grab control. In the 1800s socialists were busy at just that, in New England a fusion of Owenites, Hegelians and Unitarians. Control of Harvard was wrenched from Calvinists in 1805, largely by Unitarians, for state control; by the 1830s Horace Mann was busy "liberating" the public schools: transferring control from local communities with their "common schools" to state schools. And "The State will not surrender the right to regulate education having once attained this right . . .", Prof. Paulsen of the University of Berlin told the National Education Association (NEA) in 1906.(1) It was the Puritans who had created the burgeoning society and culture, control of which power seekers schemed to grab.

The Puritans, so often denigrated and slandered today, were a great people. It was their vision of a covenanted society that provided the principal model for the government of our Founders, as even Hannah Arendt has confirmed.(2) They have been abused for "witch hunting", for bigotry and the like, which is a gross calumny by those who were themselves bigots. A 1940 thesaurus lists under "bigot": Pharisees, iconoclast; a 1985 thesaurus has "Puritan" substituted for "Pharisee". If it was morally wrong to use the historical, or biblical word "Pharisee", then it was an egregious hate crime and an attack upon society to replace it with Puritan, so essential in our history.

By late 17th century witchcraft was recognized as a delusion which had arisen earlier in Europe. Puritan Cotton Mather wrote a book on how to defuse allegations. Unfortunately he described how the "possessed" were "supposed" to behave, and a group of girls from the less orderly end of Salem accused an elderly servant as a prank. She was flogged and the girls felt forced to reveal others, and still more; some of the accused pointed to others to free themselves. What had started as a springtime prank by fall had grown to accusations against the wives of even the leaders. That was when, of course, rationality took hold.

Fourteen women and five men had been hanged (none burned), four died in jail, fifty-five saved themselves by accusing others. Only one man, Giles Corey, refused to play the game; to force him he was pressed, crushed, until he died. The entire court was disbanded and 150 released. In a few years the convictions were annulled and relatives indemnified. This account comes from Harvard historian, S. E. Morison.(3)

The witch hunting had been incited by thoughtless girls, not by society at large; evil does happen, but when the stability of the community was endangered there were authorities who did step forward and stop it and indemnification was made, because there were no witches. Some fifty years ago when McCarthy was accused of witch hunting no authorities arose to demand the truth; Walter Lippmann who warned of the tyrannical collectivists in 1936 and Diana Trilling who described in the Nineties her direct experience with Communists, failed to demand the truth and indemnification, as did the Puritans.

Worse bigots have used this brief summer aberration to vilify the roots of our human society, and to force the perception that the Puritans and hence Americans were mean, evil, and narrow minded, much as most untypical My Lai in Vietnam has been used. (See Chapt. VIII, Ref. 12, p. 339-41.) The power of public opinion is the power to exclude, and to be seen to exclude; to accuse and condemn and be seen to crush, to lie and dissemble while publicly lauded. "When treason prospers, none dare call it treason".

President Truman started the exposing of Communists in sensitive positions in 1947; the famous "blacklisting" of Hollywood Communists in 1947 was forced not by government nor capitalism but by public demand. Edward Dmytryk of the "Hollywood Ten", was soon to "realize that in joining with Stalinists as defenders of the Bill of Rights he had been complicit in a terrible hoax". FDR and Truman could speak of "good old Joe" Stalin, but to suggest "good old Joe" McCarthy is unspeakable, claiming McCarthy far more evil than Stalin -- just as anti-Communism was forced to be perceived as more evil than Communism. The accusation of witch hunting was a blatant attempt to force the perception that there were likewise no Communists. But it has been the liberals, all the way from the far left to the "moderates" of both parties who supported and continue to uphold that evil lie. Witness after witness, and documents from Gouzenko's to *Verona*, prove the infestation and corruption of Communism was worse than McCarthy claimed. But there has been no apologies to the McCarthy and other families, and no indemnification. A McCarthy scourge, Ellen Schrecker, blundered into the truth: it "was not his bluster but his anti-Communism". The real evil is not in condemning McCarthy; it is in supporting the Communists, renegades, the deadly enemies of their own society, freedoms, and future.

Horace Mann, the celebrated "educator", had in the 1840s initiated a vehement struggle to wrest control of education, and hence of culture and all of society, into the hands of a socialist regime. The intent to do so was announced at the NEA convention of 1871. G. Stanley Hall, also in 1871, returned from studying socialism in Germany, and was later to write, "I fairly loathed and hated so much of America . . . it was fortunate that . . . (this) result was never openly expressed and my socialist leanings (remained) unknown . . . I should have been barred from any academic career".(4) Conspiracy.

Hall went to Johns Hopkins to teach, and John Dewey as one of his first students absorbed Hall's hatred with a deep but unexpressed enthusiasm. Dewey went on to the University of Chicago where, from 1894 to 1904, he developed his ideas on education in a Laboratory School. He aimed to create among students a social spirit, requiring cooperative classroom activities. "It is a great mistake to make reading and writing constitute the bulk of school work . . . It is not claimed that with the method suggested (his whole-word or look-say, to replace phonics) the child will learn to read as much or as readily".(5) Dewey expressed his intent more clearly later, "The first great step . . . is to inform students about present society . . . in such a way that enables them . . . to take an active part in aggressively . . . bringing about a new social order".(6) "It is now proposed to bureaucratize (socialize) the educational system of the whole United States, while making the most solemn assurances that nothing of the kind is intended", so wrote Nicholas Murray Butler, Dewey's president at Columbia University to his Board of Governors in 1921. Conspiracy?

A network of socialist cells had been formed by Dewey and others in our major universities by 1900. David Tyack in his *Managers of Virtue*(7) described its tremendous power in public education. "Reform" was promoted by "educationalists" to wrest control of education from local authorities. They gained control of "money, reputations, placement of students and friends, training of future leaders, and influence over professional organizations and civil, legislative and administrative bodies".(8) And what happened to "disloyal subordinates": "Give 'em the ax": (Strayer's Law, at Teachers College, Columbia).(9)

The socialist network had expanded into the NEA's Representative Assembly by 1921, enormously influencing teachers in 463 local associations through the NEA *Journal* (1922). By 1930 it had coerced publishers into printing only "primers" based on Dewey's whole-word method of learning to read. But already Dr. S. T. Orton, a neuropathologist specializing in speech and reading disorders in many large systems that he studied, warned that look-say, or the whole-word method, "often proves an actual obstacle to reading progress and . . . may prevent acquisition of an academic education for children of average capacity . . . may also give rise to far reaching damage to their emotional life".(10) Exactly what would be repeatedly documented over the next seventy years.

To comprehend the situation it is necessary to recognize that the whole-word method or learning to read was developed in 1830 by T.H. Gallaudet for teaching reading to the deaf and dumb. Such people cannot hear sounds and syllables; hence are unable to use memory of the sounds in learning to read or to spell, a far older coding for communications than symbolic encoding. The whole-word method must depend solely upon the memorizing of symbols, as hieroglyphs. Phonics depends on the brain's powerful ability to remember sounds, in addition to quick recognitions by sight. It also provides an essential assist to spelling and pronunciation.

By 1936 "nearly a half million children with reading disabilities", declared the NEA *Journal*(11); Dewey had admitted that the whole word was an inferior method. In 1947, "Millions of children suffer from dyslexia", in *Life Magazine*.(12) In 1955 Dr. Rudolf Flesch published *Why Johnny Can't Read*(13); it was look-say, and Flesch pointed a finger. The NEA fired back, "Deliberately attempting to mislead and deceive the people . . ." In 1965 President Johnson provided a billion dollars for "remedial reading", a growth industry. When I started to school in a one-room, prairie school in 1927, there was no "remedial reading"; anyone with only three or four years of schooling, like my father, knew how to read. He read voraciously, on significant social issues.

Dr. Jeanne Chall at Harvard's Graduate School of Education published in 1967, *Learning to Read*.(14) From the "belly of the beast" it was written to, not about, her colleagues; it pointed no fingers. Years of intensive research and mountains of data had convinced her that the phonics system of learning to read was much superior to the whole-word method. A reviewer gave the NEA's reply in the *Journal of Reading*. Chall's studies "were ill-conceived, incomplete and lacking in . . . methodological criteria . . . personal bias . . . (had) moored her on a reef of inconclusiveness and insubstantiality . . . (she had) failed to achieve respectability".(15) *Pravda* couldn't have said it better. The NEA, like their friends the Communists, found that a sneer was the best response to an uncomfortable truth. When the facts are against you, attack motive, character, anything to change the subject. And the bottom line is that he who is with the "mainstream", controlling public perceptions, can always win.

The challenges of Orton, Flesch, Chall, and others were simply ignored by the NEA and media. Marva Collins, as unaccredited, was allowed only to substitute in Chicago a few years back, but she replaced the "See Spot run, run, run" look-say readers with fables -- Aesops's and Fontaine's -- and story books, and she taught phonics. The "run, run, run" books will disgust any child; she taught children in Chicago's worst schools to read, and to read with relish the stories of real feelings of joy, greed, malice, and the failure of evil.(16) Donna Connell's(17) kindergartners learned to read, regardless of IQ or economic background. But at Dewey's special Lincoln School (at Columbia), which the Rockefeller boys attended, biographer Jules Abel reported, "Lawrence did not (learn) to read and write . . ." and Nelson admitted that reading was "slow and tortuous".(18)

Even as Dewey's monster continues devouring young lives, others are retrieved. Suzanne Chazin told in *Readers*

Digest of 38 year-old Andy, unable to comprehend letters as determining sounds and spelling. At one of her lessons, on the word "blend", she let the word roll "B - lll - end". Andy repeated, "B - lll - and . . . Blandy . . . Andy! I can hear the sounds . . . like my name!" Andy was hooked on phonics. Think of the millions of "retards", hooked in "Remedial" with billions in tax money. In Dec. 1999 the annual National Council of Teachers formally opposed phonics instruction.

In the following year Diana Ravitch's *Left Back: A Century of Failed Reforms*(19) was reviewed by Alan Wolfe. He paraphrased her book, "Imagine a small group of revolutionaries intent on taking over society (as Machiavelli and Dewey proposed). Certain that they know what is best . . . they dismiss all opposition as elitist . . . their single minded determination enables them to purge dissenters and to ignore critics". With full media support it's not difficult. "It becomes clear that Ravitch does not exaggerate", he added in *The New Republic*.(20)

Wolfe follows Ravitch into the nature v. nurture misunderstanding. Certainly there is inside each child a soul, a character, wishing to express itself (nature), but it can do so only through reasoning of what it has been taught (nurture). The nature to be sought is the Greek's "proper to man", and is included in the humanness of a culture. And *all* children deserve the opportunity to follow that search for humanness, and to be encouraged to do so as long as they will. "Nothing will ever serve them better." Recall the NEA's condemnation of Chall and her book, as "moored on a reef of inconclusiveness"; a critical letter in response to Wolfe's review charged "Ravitch and Wolfe founder(ing) on the shoals of conspiracy theories."(20A) Conspiracy again; as Schumpeter remarked, Communists and liberals have learned that a sneer will serve when there is no answer.

Peter Wagschal, professor of education at the University of Massachusetts in 1980, predicted that "sophisticated audio, video, and computer technologies will soon replace the three Rs, reading, writing and arithmetic, and citizens will be largely illiterate".(21) The idea of dumping the "three Rs" became widely circulated by an article in 1951 in the *Bulletin* of the National Association of Secondary Principals, "We've built a sort of halo around (them) . . . they were for everybody . . . rich and poor, brilliant and not so . . . We've made progress in getting rid of that slogan".(22) "The majority of American students (60 percent) are incapable of being prepared for college or (even) trained for vocations", pontificated the U.S. Office of Education.(23) Today *Goals 2000* is the continuation of the "dumbing down" effort.

John Simon in 1981 in his *Esquire* column, and in his book *Paradigms Lost*,(24) wrote a scathing denunciation of the professor and his claim. To Wagschal's assertion that "present computers can store more information, in less space and communicate more quickly and reliably than any printed matter, and the next generation will be faster, cheaper . . . calling up information instantly in response to the spoken word",(25) Simon replied, "How would an illiterate understand the computer speaking, with written language's attributes of precision and completeness which it would necessarily have to speak to convey information of any complexity"?(26) Yet MIT Professor Papert recently supported the idea, "The Terrorist Attack" proves we need to "acquire knowledge faster, sees a shift from static paper based media" and "new ways of organizing people".(27) "Organizing people", is totalitarian and the death of humanness.

This undermining of the basics is commonly given in a black context; Wagschal's announcement had as its "primary emphasis" the "black child" with a picture of Julian Bond on the cover. He goes on, "The three Rs are by their very nature, tools of the affluent and elite . . . Illiteracy of the majority of the globe's population has never been a reflection of species wide stupidity, but of the limiting nature of print. Only a minority, the elite of the globe's population can afford the time and resources required to learn and to use the three Rs".(28)

This account, presented in Reginald Damerell's *Education's Smoking Gun*,(29) along with an excellent introduction to the nature of literacy and how the mind works is most interesting and informative for anyone in the teaching trade. A few years ago, I had a Chinese girl, graduate student, doing very excellent scientific research. When she started she could barely speak English. Later, I asked her, "When you think, do you think in English or Chinese?" She replied, "Usually now I think in English, but if it is very, very difficult, I must think in Chinese".

"Our public school teachers are no longer the benign, neutral servants of our communities . . . their ability to control the minds of our youth . . . " is the power to destroy human society. "NEA will become a political power second to none . . . " has been its brag since Sam Lambert was NEA's secretary in 1967. The corruption of a once world renowned educational system to one just above Iran, South Africa, and Macedonia has been the work of the NEA and its leader, John Dewey. Dewey based his new American education on the belief that " . . . (T)ruth and facts are so exclusively individual . . . tending to pass into selfishness . . . (there is) no social motive for acquirement of mere learning . . . " And "language is not primarily the expression of thought, but a means of communication".

This is the core of NEA education; mass youth is to be brought up as clients of the regime, with whom it would need only to communicate, not as reasoning human beings. A youth driven only by feelings is an animal; reasoning from truth of a culture is the basis of humanness. The liberal poet W.H. Auden declared speech "as a code of communication" to be subordinate "to speech in the true sense, the medium in which we as unique persons who think . . . gratuitously disclose ourselves . . . "(30)

The famous Coleman Report, commissioned by President Johnson in 1965 under the new Civil Rights Act, explained that public education had become like a socialized economy, where inputs and outputs had become totally unrelated.(31)   Only one significant factor stood out: teachers' scores on a vocabulary test, conducted by the study. A few years back Boston spent $9,000 per annual student, while Detroit was near the national average of about $4,500, yet the drop-out rate of each was nearly the same, nearly 50 percent, and as is common less than half of the *high school seniors* read at 8th grade level.

Al Shanker, long head of the AFL's teachers union (union in both Boston and Detroit) declared that "Ninety-five percent of those *who go to college* in the U.S. would not be admitted anywhere else . . . " An excellent report by Chubb and Moe of the liberal Bookings Institution, urged get rid of "public schools", unions, and the credentialing of teachers. They gave "page after page" of evidence, as in Coleman's report, of the importance of "family education", in determining *attitudes* toward responsibility, discipline, and a desire to learn, summarized in the *Atlantic Monthly*.(32)

Three of the greatest corruptions of public education today are "outcome-based education", sex education, and computers. OBE is a cruel fraud; its outcomes refer to higher order thinking in the "affective domain", related to prejudice, environmentalism, gender, the "homeless", with group study, no standards, grades, or discipline. Sex-ed was designed and has been perfected, admittedly, to abolish family and human society.   Then there is the "computer cult", designed and promoted by entrepreneurs who know and care less about education, claiming that computers can teach something that traditional teaching cannot, and that they bring resources beyond that ever before possessed.   Actually storing knowledge (facts) permits and enables your brain computer to make comparisons, draw relations, develop ideas more powerfully, faster and more generally than any computer. Human memory is the food of thought, the larger it is the richer and more complex can be the mind's creative processes.   These are assertions of nearly all computer specialists at MIT, Harvard, and elsewhere; read "The Myth of Computers" in *The New Republic*,(33) and "Computer Cult",

Chronicles, (34) and also *The Dilemma of Education*, by R. Powers.(35)

John Dewey had other "progressive" interests; he encouraged Morris Cohen at Harvard to develop his proposal for "judicial legislation", which Cohen presented in 1913. By 1935, son Felix wrote in a paper, "Socialism and the Myth of Legality",(36) that no part of law or Constitution could not be set aside by the Court, and he pointed admiringly to Hitler's success in doing just that. So began the final stage of the long and persistent struggle by the regime's intellectuals to pry off the restraints of law, of rule-of-law; an intent-less Constitution would provide the necessary fulcrum.

The principal concern of the drafters of our Constitution was to provide barriers to power-grasping by a bureaucracy of the national State, and also to reckless actions by the masses. Their *intent* was stated very precisely by the principal author of the Constitution, James Madison; "All that concerns the lives, the liberties, and the properties of the people" was to be the business and concern *only* of the people in their local governments. This is stated most emphatically in "Congress shall make no law" of the First Amendment, and "retained by the people", and "reserved to the States or to the people", in the Ninth and Tenth.

The first threat came quickly; in 1798, French Jacobins sought to engage people in the new nation in talk and actions considered as dangerous to social stability, particularly when associated with an indigenous political party. This resulted in the passage of the contentious and dubious Alien and Sedition Acts. Then in 1807 Jefferson's Embargo Act led to shipping restrictions particularly detrimental to New England, and demands for relief quickly escalated into calls for secession, by New England in 1809.

The difference in the economies of North and South, with resulting different effects of trade, led in 1838 to the passage of the "tariff of abomination", and in response to that tariff came demands for nullification or secession in the South. The South was agricultural, aristocratic, dispersed, while the North was entrepreneurial, shopkeeping, and organized. The tariff reduced the price which foreign buyers would pay Southern producers for their products and increased the price of Southern purchases, while sheltering Northern industries from foreign competition. The South up until about 1830 had a growing movement for ending slavery, but the North not only failed to aid the effort, either by promoting even minor proposals for compensation, or by offering to help to solve the problems raised by the liberation of a class of people totally unable to be equal economically, politically, or technically, barely a generation from a "stone age".

Instead the behavior of the North was most disgraceful. "Abolitionists and others", wrote Yankee historian J.T. Adams, (37) "by their intemperate and often untrue denunciations of the South sought to instill into Northern minds a hatred of the South and its people greater than for slavery itself". The source of the imposed vehemence was early socialists, much as fifty years ago liberals created an imposed hatred for anti-Communists greater than for Communists, and it still exists. The Northern abolitionists, who learned their hatred from Fourier and Lassalle socialists, smugly told the South that the solution was to end slavery and their cotton export problem would disappear.

The Abolitionist leadership cared little for the Negro: let the South "take one way, and we t'other"(38). Lincoln himself said in 1854 in answer to Judge Douglas; "I will not blame (the South) for not doing what I should not know how to do myself . . . free them . . . politically and socially our equals? My feelings will not admit this . . . (and) those of the great mass of people will not . . . (which) cannot be safely disregarded. We cannot make them our equal".(39)

Boston historian Adams continued, "The right to hold slaves was strongly imbedded in the Constitution . . . "(40), in contradiction to so much race propaganda today about the evil of Judge Taney and others. To end the institution of slavery was the responsibility of all people, and all sections, to accomplish by *compromise*. Instead Wendell Phillips called the Union "accursed of God"(41), and "the Reverend" Theodore Parker and Wm. Lloyd Garrison in his *The Liberator*, urged "kill without compunction". "They were neither statesmen nor humanitarians but madmen bent in burning down . . . in order that their fanaticism might prevail".(42) "We shall see the terrible results of joining this group of fanatics with others in the history of reconstruction."(43)

The following account of Constitutional Reconstruction is based largely on Horace Flack's classic, *The Adoption of the Fourteenth Amendment,* 1908.(44)

Radical Republicans in the Congress had been unable to do much to punish the South while Lincoln was winning the war, but his assassination provided the spark and the warrant for an attack, claiming it to be a Southern crime. The hatred couldn't be allowed to flag, even though the South was prostrate, devastated, starving, and without operating civil institutions.

The extreme vehemence of the Radicals sprang from a fear, the visible horror of a reunited Democratic Party that would have a majority in Congress, *and* in the Electoral College. The fanatical leader of the Radicals, Thaddeus Stevens, announced a solution: the Southern states, despite the fact that they had nearly all been "reconstructed" by Lincoln's program, "ought never to be recognized as valid states until the Constitution shall have been amended . . . as to secure perpetual ascendancy" for the Republican party!(45) Granting Negro suffrage would not do because few Northern states allowed Negroes, or even Irishmen, to vote.

The plan was to begin by declaring that Southern delegations to Congress would not be allowed to take their seats. Even though Southern states had been recognized, by being asked and by providing their votes for passage of the

13th Amendment ending slavery, they now, a year after the war's end would be disenfranchised. The Radicals knew that their planned 14th Amendment would certainly be blocked in Congress if the Southern delegations were seated. Even a Republican Senator from New Jersey, known to be hostile to the 14th, was ejected from the Senate in order to insure a two thirds vote for passage. A fear began to flicker that the Bill of Rights would be repealed.

The blackest days of the American republic were to follow. The proposed amendment, in the formulation of which a large group of states had been illegally denied participation and lacking a Constitutionally required presidential signature, was submitted to the states for passage. When most of the Southern states rejected the Amendment, thus blocking its passage, the Radical's fury rose. They passed a Reconstruction Act, ordering a full military occupation of the South, nearly two years after the end of the war and with Presidential reconstruction nearly complete. Puppet governments were installed by the military in all the Southern states; the President was impeached and pushed aside with the Tenure Act which denied him the Cabinet, and the Supreme Court was terrorized into declaring the Court incompetent in "political matters". Thad Stevens held total power.

While Congress was forcing recisions on the 14th's defeat in the Southern states by carpet-bagger legislatures, it was denying to Northern states, the right of recision as they became aware of the great harm that the 14th Amendment would inflict on Constitutional protections.

The unconstitutional adoption of the feculent 14th was a mortal attack upon human society. The so-called Slaughterhouse Cases of 1873 temporarily seemed to provide some recovery but it was more guile that real. By 1886 one of the renegades who had helped hatch the 14th stood before a corrupt Court (Southern Pacific, 118, U.S. 394) and reckoned that they'd had in mind "that corporations were people when they wrote it". Consequently, states' power to curb the growing excesses of corporations was thereby denied as illegal by this new 14th. The so-called evils of capitalism are seldom inherent in the market, or in the abstraction of "capitalism"; they are commonly the evils of corrupt men in government.

But this restriction of state power, important as it is, is overshadowed by what was to become the full activation of the feculent 14th. It was addressed to "All persons", and "No State" . . . "shall deprive any person", and finally "Congress shall have power . . . " Thus the true and only "wall of separation" in the Constitution: between "the lives, liberties and properties of the people" and the national State was breached, and the national State was empowered to enter and to become the supreme conferrer and judge of all rights, all policies, all perceptions. That exalted position, conferred upon the people in their local governments by the Founders, was now grasped by the regime of an empowered State in the name of giving "rights" to the people, which would soon become a mere forbearance.

During and following WW I the media and the Court forced the perception that the nature of free speech would be defined by that regime. Later the power to define free press, free exercise of religion, and assembly would also be asserted by that increasingly tyrannical regime. Rule-of-law would be vaporized under an intentless-Constitution. The regime in the media would declare through the Court that socialist propaganda could replace law and would identify the enemies, as well as the privileged, of the State. And there would be no significant power to halt this totalitarianism.

Some of these usurpations were to come after WW II, but as has been noted, Lippmann and many others had by 1936 recognized that rule-of-law and self government were things of the past. And after Roosevelt's "court packing" scheme, judges reevaluated their position: if the President could be supported in such corruption by the media, they could assert their own authority similarly.

The Constitution specifically and intentionally limited the Supreme Court to an appellate function, but Justice Louis Brandeis developed and forced the introduction of additional evidence at the Supreme Court level with a corresponding bloating of powers with the renouncing of that limitation.

Justice is a very ancient, even pre-historic, concept from natural law. It is known to all people and depends upon no written law. The great jurist Learned Hand, long denied appointment to the Supreme Court warned us: "Liberty lies in the hearts of men and women; when it dies there, no Constitution, no law, no court can save it." In fact it never really dies; it can be awakened. It is the greatest human duty of each of us today to arouse it.

VIII CONSPIRACY

To conspire is to join secretly usually to do a wrongful act. Clearly based on deceit and lies, the intent is to undermine, to subvert that which cannot be attacked openly. Modernity in its entirety is one vast conspiracy, based on Machiavelli's "demonic dream" of an intellectuals' total regime.

The conspiracy of modernity is unique, paradoxical, and much in need of study. The Reasoners vowed to replace religion with the loose cannon of unpurposed reason, the Enlighteners to unloose the bonds of society -- for an anomic individualism!; then the Communists and liberals openly planned to eradicate families, rule of law (with an "intentless" Constitution), and education in self government. Everybody knows who these people are today, and what they are about. A conspiracy in the open, but everybody pretends not to see. There is no real secrecy, no concealment, except of the very inner recesses of the regime unknown even to loyal followers.

Communists and intellectual enemies of human society have evolved a number of evasive tactics, two of which have been noted. The "guffaw" serves in place of a refutation for an unpleasant truth; at other times a "sneer" will do, as for example at a "conspiracy theory". Thus, a TV program on Pearl Harbor prepared for the 50th Anniversary revealed rather surprisingly and openly Franklin Roosevelt's treacherous "day of infamy". It was harshly condemned in a *Wall Street Journal* review by Dorothy Rabinowitz(1), for "accusatory testimony, suspicions, insinuations . . . of revisionists and conspiracy theorists", accusing Franklin Roosevelt of "sacrificing those killed at Pearl Harbor to his war aims." She pinpoints the "America Firsters" as the "terminal right", thus Nazis, fascists; on the other hand was the "fashionable Left". "Pearl Harbor", she continued, "was a particularly bitter day for American Firsters"; presumably a good day for the "fashionable Left". But who made the Communists so "fashionable", when 85 percent of Americans was America First in spirit? Her indignation and spleen arose from the "accusatory conspiracy theory", and no one objected to its sheer fatuosity.

Then more recently there was Hillary. In the face of the fetid capaciousness of "her husband's" alleged depravity and criminal cover-ups, she took TV time to blame America for a "vast right wing conspiracy". Some slow-witted wondered how she could be taken seriously. That was, however, never an intention; the intention was to create a "perception". And "perceptions are as important as reality" (even more so), "regardless of the facts involved". So claimed UAW Chief, Doug Fraser, according to a *Detroit News* editorial a few years back.

"Image-makers like to play around with perceptions" as a sneaky way "to manipulate people", or news. That's why "facts or rational arguments" are considered inferior "to perceptions"; the latter are "socially constructed", while the former are as illusory as truth. Racism, anti-Semitism, patriarchy, and conspiracy are some of today's controlling "perceptions". And he who controls the media controls all "socially constructed", and hence rules all. Over the past century particularly since 1936 when Lippmann discerned the control of a collectivist establishment or regime it has been resisted even significantly from time to time, but our slide into Statism has never been more than momentarily slowed.

In 1938 Franklin Roosevelt urged New Dealer Congressman Martin Dies of Texas to form, and to chair, a committee on Un-American Activities. Roosevelt had only "fascists" in mind, and Dies did investigate those few who could be found. However, the real action was among Lippmann's collectivists, the Communists; they were plentiful and feisty. Dies had watched in disbelief as FDR gave recognition to the Stalinist regime in the Soviet in 1933, even as millions of peasant carcasses stunk on the plains of the Ukraine. The Soviets had promised that they would not allow subversive groups to operate in the U.S., but very shortly the

Communist International announced it would do just that, and assured the comrades that the signed scrap of paper would be lost in the relations that would develop.(2)

And sure enough it was soon open-house at the White House; Earl Browder, the Communists's General Secretary, came and went frequently. Eleanor enjoyed entertaining young Communist leaders. Eventually Lauchlin Currie came to reside in the White House; while perhaps not a party member, he was in deep enough to need to skip off to South America after Roosevelt died. And Harry Hopkins whom Verona characterized as Stalin's principal agent also lived there.

Roosevelt's war provocations led to opposition groups urging non-involvement, the most influential being the "America First Committee" created in early 1940. Prominent members were Senators Wheeler and Nye, Charles Lindberg, Robert Wood of Sears Roebuck, the *New Republic* writer John T. Flynn, NRA director Hugh Johnson, Gerald Ford, Potter Stewart, John L. Lewis' daughter Kathryn, and many more. The fact is that 85 percent of Americans were America First in spirit and looked to them for leadership. It is bigotry and racist to stigmatize them as Nazi, belittling and untrue to denigrate them as isolationists. They were predominately anti-totalitarian, as those who attacked them were not and are not, being invariably friends of Communism. Other less well known anti-Communist groups of churches and women's organizations, were given an intended-to-be derogatory title in *Women of the Far Right and WW II*, a book by Glen Jeansonne a Jewish writer biased toward a crypto-communism who has nevertheless provided a rather fair and forceful account of them. Also a group of some 50 prominent individuals signed a forceful blast against Roosevelt's illegal and subversive war policies; signers varied from liberal President Hutchins of the University of Chicago to opera star Geraldine Farrar, from WW I Gen. Davies to New Dealer Felix Morley, and from Herbert Hoover to Irving S. Cobb.

Conspiracy rests on lies. Roosevelt's diabolical plan to

use America's blood and treasure to empower Communism around the world (Chapter VI, ref. 2), and thereby destroy Western civilization, would have startled Marx and Lenin. Central to the lies concerning the origin of this catastrophe are the two critical years from mid-1939 to mid-1941, marking the Stalin-Hitler Alliance era. The significant "isolationists" of influence were supporters of Communism, who denounced "American imperialism", devised work stoppages in defense plants, and were the effective opponents of preparedness.(3) They were openly sympathetic to their Nazi ally, while the America Firsters opposed all totalitarianism.

It was Franklin Roosevelt's deranged obsession to save Communism, which induced him to sacrifice the lives of thousands of young men and the Pacific Fleet, just to get involved, and then America's self-governing human society and Western civilization in the struggle. This was made visible in his message of "Cause" to Churchill in early January, 1941, while Stalin and Hitler were still allies in a "war of aggression" against democratic Europe. His infatuation and frenzy became much more directed after Stalin was attacked on June 22, 1941; on June 24 he announced that Lend Lease would be extended to Stalin.(4) On July 25, he cut off all supplies to Japan, froze their assets and closed the Panama Canal to Jap shipping.

The lies and dissemblings about this period are beyond most people's imaginations. Clare Boothe Luce declared "He lied us into war." Even more culpable are the continuing deceptions to cover the treachery and lies. Typical is S.E. Morison's account in his *Oxford History of American People*, which is excellent up to WW I. Never once is mentioned the frantic calls to Roosevelt by both Japanese Premier Prince Konoye and the American Ambassador Joseph Grew. Hull's ultimatum and Magic intercepts had been known for nearly two decades when Morison's history was published, yet are unmentioned. A Churchill spokesman declared in 1944, "(I)t is a travesty of history to say that America was forced into war . . . America provoked . . . the Japanese to attack", a truth never hinted. All unmentioned in the mainstream.

It was early in 1941 as FDR was declaring his "Cause" for Stalin when he also began to exhort an unreceptive Attorney General Biddle into going after the America Firsters, who were using their rights to attack his war policies in peacetime. (Vietnam War renegades attacked far beyond policies; they attacked government, and law, and America, in wartime!) The America First protestors were against not America or its government but against FDR's war and his siding with totalitarianism. No conspiracy; it was neither secret nor lies. After June 22, 1941 (the date Stalin was attacked by Hitler), leftist prosecutor Maloney began rounding up "seditionists",(5) though the country was at peace and faced no real threat.

Franklin Roosevelt's "Great Sedition Trial" began with 28 indictments on July 21, 1942, charging a conspiracy to violate the sedition sections of the 1917 Espionage Act and the peacetime "Alien Registration Act", known as the Smith Act of 1940.(6) The second indictments with six names added, of Jan., 1943, came largely because of the failure of the first, as nearly all previously enumerated conspiracy acts predated passage of the Smith Act. A new prosecutor was named: O. John Rogge, a defense lawyer for Communist supporters, including David Greenglass in the Rosenberg atom spy case. Active in many Communist fronts, he had been entertained by Stalin and Vyshinsky in the Kremlin after laying a wreath in Red Square.

The Jewish owned *Washington Post* played a major role in forcing the indictments and in orchestrating the trial; it "loaned" reporter Dillard Stokes to the joint FBI-ADL (Jewish Anti-Defamation League) investigation team. Dillard, under the assumed name, "Jefferson Breen", had written requests to the numerous defendants asking for copies of their literature, to be sent to an address in Washington, D.C. Thus it was that separate individuals from all over the country, could be dragged to Communist infested Washington D.C. for four years to stand trial on conspiracy, though few were even aware of each other. The majority were poor individuals from small communities, unable to afford a lawyer; some were allegedly insane. It was a manifest injustice, and indicative of the fundamental unscrupulosity of the Rooseveltian regime, that dared not take on the powerful Father Coughlin, Charles Lindbergh, or Senator Wheeler, whose attacks on FDR's war policies were far more telling; instead they vented their hatred on little people, and accused the leaders of anti-Semitism.

Henry Klein was the Jewish defense lawyer for Eugene Sanctuary who with his wife ran a Presbyterian foreign mission in New York and had written "several hundred" sacred or patriotic songs -- one, "Uncle Sam We Are Standing By You", published in June, 1942. Another of his defendants, Elmer J. Garner of Kansas, 83 years old, a great-grandfather of three, nearly stone deaf, was Vice President Nance Garner's first cousin. Senator Langer described him to the Senate: "The mailing permit for his weekly paper had been taken from him; he lived with his aged wife through small donations, keeping a goat, chickens, and raising vegetables on his small plot. Held in a (Washington) jail for several weeks for lack of bond, impoverished by three indictments and forced trips and stays in Washington . . ." He died alone in a Washington flophouse, bent over his typewriter typing his defense, with 40 cents in his pocket. The government kept his clothing and his typewriter; his naked body was freighted back to Kansas in a wooden box, so that clothes had to be purchased for his funeral. Henry Klein opened his case with an attack:

WE WILL SHOW this prosecution was undertaken to cover the crimes of the government . . . in opposition to Attorney General Biddle.

WE WILL PROVE the persecution was instigated by professional Jews who prey on other Jews   by scaring them . . . with threatened pogroms, (and that) anti-Semitism charged in the indictment is a racket run by racketeers for graft.

WE WILL SHOW that the most vicious attacks on Jews and on the Roosevelt administration (remember Mr. Klein was a Jew) emanated from the office of the FBI, by one of its agents . . . to provoke others to do likewise.

(Auguring of Oklahoma, Waco, Ruby Ridge.)

WE WILL SHOW this agent drilled his underlings in New York with broomsticks, preparatory to "killing Jews".

In Paquita de Shishmaroff, or "Mady", a well-to-do American-born widow of a Czarist officer, Mr. Rogge ran into a buzz saw. She was sharp, never pushy but knew how to use men, a formidable opponent. She had supplied Henry Ford's *Dearborn Independent* with its stories on Jewish power. She was vociferously anti-Semitic, but that was her only "crime". She was quickly excused. Mrs. Dilling was another; an articulate author and lecturer from Chicago, she was highly regarded as a leader in anti-Communism. Senator Langer often visited the defendants in jail, and frequently escorted Mrs. Dilling in and out of the courts. She had committed "sedition" by reprinting in her newsletter a speech given in Congress by Rep. Clare Hoffman in which an America soldier in the Philippines was quoted as complaining, ostensibly dangerous to military morale, that his outfit lacked bombers because they had been given to Britain and the Soviet.

The government worked with unlimited funds and facilities, while most of the indicted were very poor people totally unfamiliar with the "big-time". Paquita or "Mady", wrote that "their physical lives were made almost impossible", with little to eat and hamstrung in every way. Ernest Elmhurst got a job as a waiter to help pay his expenses, but Walter Winchell learned of it and agitated over his widely-heard broadcast to get him fired. Two defense attorneys had shots fired at them; one lost a twelve year law association; another was beaten by five thugs and hospitalized for five days. Henry Klein was viciously harassed, held in contempt, ultimately driven from the case for contempt -- later overruled.

A picture of an incident at the trial was sketched by defendant Otto Brennemann, showing prosecution (sic) witness Henry Allen breaking down on the stand, as his two attractive twin daughters rushed to his aid. He had been describing how he and his son had been brutalized and beaten, to the point of blinding one eye of his son, by what Allen described as "Jewish Communists".

They were nevertheless generally a feisty bunch: a sign painter 80 percent deaf, a Detroit factory worker, a waiter and a maid. A German-American poet and social critic, George Viereck (well-known foreign publicist for the German government as far back as 1916), was on trial when his son died in combat as an American soldier. Rich and poor shared sorrows, consorted together. One day after the prosecutor had read off the names of administration officials whom the "seditionists" had attacked, one shouted out, "Don't forget Eleanor!"

FDR sought to intimidate America by attacking the generally weak and defenseless. He did not dare to take on Lindbergh, or Senator Wheeler, journalist John Flynn, or even Father Coughlin.

Then a defense attorney for Ernest Elmhurst lit the fuse. He demanded in open court that the ADL-B'nai B'rith files be impounded as evidence, insisting that it would be impossible to proceed without them. It was obvious, and known to all, that the Jewish owned *Washington Post* had played a major role, along with the ADL, in gathering evidence and pushing the indictments. Walter Winchell was another major Jewish media figure promoting the prosecution, along with Arnold Forster, ADL's New York counsel and sleuth. According to Neal Gabler, Winchell's biographer, Forster drafted entire columns for Winchell, appeared at his radio station to edit the broadcasts. They often acted as a conduit to the FBI for information on the trial. This illegal quasi-governmental role of ADL has been assumed time and again, most nefariously and recently in the vast Southern "black church-burning" hoax.

But in the Sedition Trial, the *Post* now clutched; a Jewish-American confrontation was dreaded. "We fear", they editorialized, "whatever may be the outcome of the trial, it will stand as a black mark against American justice for years to come". Barely a dozen years later, one of John Kennedy's *Profiles In Courage* was of GOP hopeful Robert Taft. "The Nuremberg Trials", wrote Taft, "will forever remain a blot on . . . American jurisprudence". Over and over Communist renegades are found ravaging law and justice.

The defendants, a diverse lot, had only one belief in common: that it was not the moral duty of Americans to squander lives and wealth to save the British and Soviet empires. They were not isolationists, they were anti-totalitarianists; they were not anti-Semitic, they were anti-Communists. Freedom House placed full page ads in the *New York Times* (January, 1943) denouncing "isolationism". The real interference with defense work by isolationists was by the crypto-Communists during the 1939-1941 Stalin-Hitler Pact period. The "sedition" case marked the totalitarian trend of convicting people and sentencing them for political beliefs; and this was to be a "Good War", to end the idea that the State should order how people were to think.

The *agent provocateur* John Roy Carlson in his book, *Under Cover* (1943), pushed the criminalization of opposition to government. Avedis Derounian was his real name; he popularized the "perception" that the America Firsters, and the American common people generally, sought fascism as their ultimate goal; America First was "a spearhead aimed at the heart of democracy", in Derounian's *Under Cover*. Such drivel was "probably written or edited by the ADL", claimed historian Richard Gid Powers in his *Not Without Honor*, on American anticommunism. When you control the media, any such nonsense becomes "public opinion." Max Lerner, Arthur Schlesinger and many more piled on. The purging of J.T. Flynn, Garet Garrett, Albert Jay Nock, Lillian Gish and many others was far more complete than the Fifties' momentary silencing of Communists. And why shouldn't the Communists have been silenced, and why purge people for anti-totalitarianism?

Sedition trial Judge E.C. Eichner, a 100 percent New Dealer, had become enraged on Nov. 30, 1944 because defendants had addressed to him envelopes stuffed with copies of Senator Langer's demand for their release. That night he went to sleep and never woke up. The *Daily Worker* fought to have the case retried. Rogge toured the nation, under B'nai B'rith auspices, seeking a continuance; it was not until June, 1947 that the Appeals Court brought it to an end, dismissing all charges. That was over two years after the "loyal Japanese-Americans" were released, three percent of whom were active traitors and twenty percent of whom demanded to be repatriated to Japan during war time. And they were not "interned", a renegade lie.

The charge made by the Communists in the Fifties that an assault on Communism was a "dagger into Franklin Roosevelt", was a typical obscurantism. It was not Roosevelt, but his sacrificing America for Stalinism that was evil. McCarthy was attacked with hate because he illegitimized "fellow travelers", contesting their fitness to serve in creating a political structure for American society. Many "conservatives" parrot the renegade's assertion that McCarthy "discredited" anti-Communism. The charge of being "discredited" for attacking evil is a fatuous contradiction in terms, like so much of liberal-left rhetoric. He had to be destroyed because he was effective. The real "harm done to anti-Communism" obviously resulted from the media's all out war on its supporters.

Anti-Communism was not a mere political expedient latched onto by McCarthy; for him it began early in his first political campaign. He did not recklessly attack innocent people; "it was not his bluster, it was his anti-Communism", blurted out Ellen Schrecker. "A most prevalent and stubborn . . . myth connected with the McCarthy era . . . is the perception that . . . any attempt to root Communists out of strategic places (forced by Truman long before McCarthy) . . . was witch hunting", wrote Sidney Hook in his *Out of Step*, p.423. "Myth" or lie? Army lawyer, Joseph Welch, whose "Have you no sense of decency, at long last sir?", while shedding Uriah

Heep tears was a contemptible act.(7) McCarthy hadn't even mentioned the name of the Communist "lad" on Welch's staff; it was the *New York Times* that had presented Fred Fisher's Communist background weeks earlier. The success of the Communist hegemony is explicit in the success of even the Communist cad Fred Fisher, and in Schrecker's admission that "Yes they did spy because they didn't subscribe to traditional forms of patriotism".

Within five years of our so-called WW II victory had come the Communist subjugation of Eastern Europe, Stalin's Berlin Blockade, Communist victory in China, revelation of atomic spies, North Korea's invasion of the South, the Alger Hiss conviction and Dean Acheson's, "I'll not turn my back . . . ". In June, 1947, the Senate Appropriations Committee gave to Secretary of State George Marshall a detailed and vigorous report on State Department security. It expressed "great alarm", backed by specifics. "It is evident that there is a deliberate, calculated program . . . not only to protect Communists in high places, but to reduce security and intelligence protection", from Democrats not McCarthy. On March 13, 1948, President Truman issued a sweeping security order forbidding agencies to provide security information to Congress. No more searching of files, interrogations, or "disclosures".

"Those who do not show anger at things that ought to arouse anger (hate) are fools", charged Aristotle. Max Eastman, former friend of Lenin, explained that "Red-baiting" was a corrupt, enforced perception used by renegades to confute the truth, to obscure their own evil policies and subvert humanness. On one hand there was scholarly ex-communist Louis Budenz who explained that condemnation of McCarthy left the way open "to intimidate any person of consequence who moved against the Communist conspiracy". On the other hand were Lenin's "useful idiots", icons of liberalism as Edward R. Murrow; in his defense of Communist Owen Lattimore he insisted on bending over backwards to be *fair.* But Murrow (one-time CBS official and head of U.S. Information Services) never hesitated to make

McCarthy look like a giggling psychopath -- even McCarthy's enemies denounced Murrow. FDR and Truman could "Good old Joe" Stalin, a real psychopathic killer; however, "Good old Joe" McCarthy was beyond toleration.

But the real target was not Joe McCarthy; to renegades seeking hegemony, McCarthyism was only a gambit, not unlike the minorities, homosexuals, families, environment and so on, all merely expendable tools. The goal was to paralyze opposition, gain unquestioned control, as revealed in many quotes, like that of leftist historian Toynbee, whose stigmatizing of "the sovereign school boards" as a "fortress of McCarthyism" was an obvious attempt to intimidate by accusation. Today, "public health is like a school of justice", recently claimed a former Harvard dean, "for redesigning society", as the public schools have long been used. No one ever explains "redesigning" for what end, and apparently no one ever asks.

"To the liberal left accepting Hiss's guilt implied renouncing hopes for Communism", wrote Allen Weinstein. David Reiff grieved "A decent feeling of mourning for a great hope . . ."(8) TV's Andy Rooney sighed for the "higher vision" of Communism. However "Communism . . . is not over, the Leninist conspiratorial approach . . . corruption by the ruling class . . . predatory secret police . . . anomic civil society . . . paranoia of public discourses . . . All these are still standing". Renegades not only "demand that others defend their right to lie about it", as Wm. Phillips, *Partisan Review* founder, charged long ago, but demand hegemonic control over society and power to criminalize all objections as hate, racist, or anti-Semitic.

McCarthy "expressed an assumption shared by millions of Americans, that our failure to obtain foreign policy goals was due to internal treason", explained former "red diaper" baby, Ronald Radosh. "The American people knew that like them, McCarthy was against Communism", by Irving Kristol in *Commentary*. "He was Joe to everyone who knew him . . . He had strength . . . courage . . . daring. Joe had a rare quality which enabled him to reach the hearts of millions . . . There was a quality which compelled respect, even from his adversaries. Some of us disagreed with him, but few were not touched by his personality", wrote Senator Lyndon Johnson in the Fifties. At a Harvard club's anniversary party (1954), a guest expressed a "gladness that Harvard had never . . . produced an Alger Hiss . . . doubly glad neither a Joe McCarthy". Senator J.F. Kennedy exploded, "How dare you couple the name of a great patriot with that of a traitor?"(9)

I have often felt similarly when the "crimes of Nixon" have been likened to those of Clinton. How terribly, terribly ignorant and unfair. Nixon's "crimes" were of a vague cover-up, in any case all directly connected with national security; bringing home half a million Americans abandoned by a perfidious Congress from a jungle hell-hole, making peace with the Chinese, and obtaining a peace treaty for Vietnam (for which the expediters were awarded Nobel Prizes), all against the constant opposition and subversion of the elite media, even churches, and much of government. Without this vehement obstruction there would have been no "plumbers", therefore no Watergate, no "Pentagon Papers", no rifling of Ellsberg's psychiatry files. On the other hand, Clinton's crimes were personal, of sex, greed, hate, corruption, suspected homicides; like FDR he used the offices of government for activities detrimental to America and to human society.

No better evidence exists for the reality of the evil power which controls our media, entertainment, even our churches, than the abject and total refusal of the Bush administration and conservatives generally even to consider investigating the crimes of the past eight years: of Waco, Oklahoma, Chinese espionage, FBI files, perjury, and Vince Foster's strange death, all cry out for the truth. If not examined out of a sense of civic decency, they should be at least as an obvious political advantage. Why are they not? Fear of the media is the only apparent answer.

In 1947, long before Joe McCarthy, Truman instituted

by executive order the first loyalty-security program opening every government employee to an FBI probe of his Americanism. The Truman Justice Department indicted and convicted the leading lights of the Communist Party of the USA, won the Dennis case and indicated the spies Judith Coplon, Alger Hiss, Wm. Remington, and Julius and Ethel Rosenberg. All were tried before Democratic judges by Democratic prosecutors and all except Coplon were upheld . . . by the Supreme Court, whose members included only one Republican, a Truman appointee." Coplon was released, as were others, rather than expose top-secret "Verona".

The U.S. National Security Agency released Verona documents in March, 1996, identifying KGB cables to Moscow from more than 100 Soviet agents employed in the Departments of State, Justice, Treasury, and OSS (pre-CIA), for 1944-45. "Liberals" hated Joe McCarthy for blaming the Democrats for "twenty years of treason". Yet Democratic Senator Moynihan would write in 1996, "We knew (from Verona) who was giving atom secrets to Soviets, we never prosecuted them . . . nor the cipher clerk who warned the Soviets we were breaking Verona. No one was indicted, all details were suppressed".(10) The guilty went well beyond those McCarthy accused. A rather moderate and recent account of McCarthy's *Life and Legacy* is available in the recent biography by Arthur Herman.(11)

McCarthy's enemies had, by their fifth investigation of him in four years, accumulated 46 counts against him; the Watkins Committee recommended he be censured on two of the counts, throwing out the other 44. The first of the two was for failing to "cooperate" in 1952 with a Senate subcommittee that had never formally subpoenaed him. This was principally in response to the previous Tydings Committee, organized to investigate disloyalty in the State Department. Tydings opened the hearing by telling McCarthy, "You occasioned this hearing, and so far as I am concerned you are going to get one of the most complete investigations ever given . . . " They never investigated the State Department at all, they attacked McCarthy. The second charge was for characterizing the Watkins hearings as "the unwitting handmaiden . . . of the Communist Party," made outside the Senate. He was "condemned" by a 65 to 22 vote on December 2, 1954.

The continuity of the collectivist's war on free society is nearly totally absent in the mainstream, in education's history, and largely even in "conservative" writings. It is readily obvious: from Dewey, Cohen, and Boas, to Lippmann's collectivist regime of 1936, then on to FDR's WW II trickery and alliance with Stalinism. It was Roosevelt's wartime Communist propaganda that ultimately forced the perception that despite Stalin's peasant holocaust, the Great Purge, Dresden, the Berlin Blockade and the subjugation of eastern Europe, that Communism was a great vision, imminent and immanent in the mainstream with Chairman Mao, and Dr. Fidel Castro in Cuba.

Early in 1956, the *NY Times'* Herb Matthews, a veteran of Communism in Spain, began taking an active interest in Cuba and Castro. By early 1957 he was on assignment -- as a "tourist" -- to meet Castro in the "rugged, impenetrable vastness of the Sierra Maestra . . . " His mission was to present Castro to the U.S. as the non-Communist, Cuban wave of the future. The capable U.S. Ambassador to Cuba, Arthur Gardner, was mysteriously replaced by an unprepared broker, Earl Smith, to confront experienced Roy Rubottom, as Asst. Sec. of State, and W.A. Wieland, of the Office of Caribbean Affairs, a Cuban native. Both had been present at the Communist uprising in Bogata, the "Bogatazo", at which Castro had been a leader.(12)

Matthews, Wieland, and Rubottom made it their task, with the *NY Times*, to force the perception in the U.S. that Cuba wanted only Castro, and in Havana that the U.S. would support only Castro. When Ambassador Smith forced his way by Rubottom to return to Washington, Wieland snared him into a press conference trap, of which a distorted version was made by the media into a great cloud of controversy: Smith had McCarthyed Castro as "Communist" -- how silly. He had not; this was but a means of smearing any opposition. Castro arrived in Havana in January, 1959 while Matthews in the *Times* praised "Dr. Fidel Castro the greatest hero." Former Ambassador Smith testified at a Senate hearing in August, 1960 that U.S. "agencies and the U.S. press played a major role in bringing Castro to power."(13)

CONSPIRACY REORGANIZED

Liberal renegades were exhilarated; anti-Communism had been stigmatized. The FBI was denied the right even to keep track of dangerous Communists, nor could they be denied employment even in defense plants. Communist direction of the U.S. government had been executed rather informally and extemporaneously by Harry Hopkins, Alger Hiss, Harry Dexter White, Lauchlin Currie, Sam Rosenman and others. To evolve an organization and a strategy, forty-six "liberals" and ten Democratic Senators initiated in 1959 the Liberal Project, and their discussions led to a book, the *Liberal Papers*.(14) Actions urged included: allowing the Soviets to plug into our early-warning defense system, unilaterally abandoning nuclear testing, dismantling NATO, withdrawal from Berlin, and neutralizing Central Europe under terms proposed by the Soviets.

However, it was not until late 1961 that Richard Barnet, of J.F. Kennedy's Arms Control Agency, and Marcus Raskin, of the National Security Council, met at a Kennedy Conference, and then resigned to become organizers and leaders of the proposed new organization. By 1963 they had incorporated the Institute for Policy Studies, which was soon to become the most important KGB stop outside of Moscow, with the help of Arthur Waskow, James Warburg, David Riesman, and Michael Maccoby. A major grant came from the Stern Family Fund, derived largely from the estate of Julius Rosenwald, a Sears, Roebuck magnate. Uncle Alfred Stern had to skedaddle behind the Iron Curtain in 1958. The Sam Rubin family, whose money came allegedly from stealing the name "Faberge", was also a contributor, as was the Mott Foundation, the Funding Exchange (IBM, Pillsbury, Gulf Western, DuPont), Ford

Foundation, and World Council of Churches. IPS also used the resources and experience of the Arthur Waskow Peace Research Institute and Playboy Foundation.(15)

The intentions of IPS have never been disguised, except in the "mainstream" where it is never identified. It set out to destroy the "Atlantic Community . . . as obsolete and dangerous, and to serve as a cover for intrigue and political agitators", and thus to provide an organization for the new "establishment" identified by Lippmann in 1936. Paul Jacobs was in favor of violent overthrow; the Black Panthers were advised and supported, as was Tom Hayden, SDS, SNCC, CORE, and Stokley Carmichael. The *Washington Examiner* described IPS as the "center which trains extremists to incite violence".

IPS served two principal functions: to provide socially destructive propaganda, as the *Vietnam Reader* declaring America evil and *Call to Resist* on draft dodging, and serving as the main source of anti-American information on the Vietnam War in the *New York Times* op-ed and elsewhere. It organized seminars, often with KGB speakers which were attended by journalists, and Congressmen and staffs. IPS helped Daniel Ellsberg leak the *Pentagon Papers* to the Soviets and to the *New York Times*. An unrivalled source of information on America's mid-century disasters, from Herb Matthews of the **New York Times** aiding Castro to power in Cuba, the Diems' (actually Ngos') assassinations, the Pentagon Papers, to the scourging of Nixon, is Russ Braley's *Bad News of the New York Times*.(16)

The second function of IPS was to provide guidance first and funding second to radical organizations and efforts. They were instrumental in promoting "Students for a Democratic Society" (SDS) and, for example, in organizing riots at Kent State, long before the excuse of Cambodia. IPS had associates in both the National Council of Churches and the World Council. IPS Fellow P. Nesbitt was an executive officer of a WCC "Program to Combat Racism", which was discredited as Communist slanted by CBS in *"60 Minutes"*. *Reader's Digest* exposed WCC's support of Marxist liberation movements and terrorists with millions of church dollars. Cora Weiss, an avowed Communist supporter in Vietnam and Latin America and wife of IPS chairman and not a Christian, led work on NCC programs. IPS is a 501(C)(3) organization receiving tax-free contributions. The Victor Rabinowitz Foundation, another IPS supporter, was headed by young Victor; as a lawyer in the Rabinowitz law office he defended Soviet spies, Judith Coplon and Alger Hiss, and served as president of the National Lawyers Guild, cited by Congress as the "Chief legal counsel and bulwark of the Communist Party".

Students for a Democratic Society became important after Lee Webb, founder of the IPS spinoff of Conference on Alternatives State Local Public Polices (CASLP), became SDS national chairman in 1963. The Weathermen, an SDS offshoot, directed the "Days of Rage" of rioting, burning, overturning cars, smashing windows in October, 1968. The Weathermen took credit for over two dozen bombings in Washington -- at the Capitol, Pentagon, and other government buildings. No terrorists; they were "peace demonstrators".

Daniel J. Bernstein, founder of DJB Foundation willed a million dollars to IPS declaring the "chief enemy of mankind is the injustice of the government of the United States". Paul Warnke, director of U.S. Arms Control, served as an IPS trustee. IPS created another spinoff (CNSS) to block intelligence gathering, and to assist KGB agent Philip Agee.

Dispatch News Service, another IPS spinoff, was created for the purpose of disinformation and discrediting of U.S. policies. Australian journalist, Communist Wilfred Burchett, wrote stories of U.S. "atrocities" in Vietnam for Dispatch; he received a steady income directly from the Kremlin. Alaskan Senator Gravel, instrumental in leaking the top-secret "Pentagon Papers", received help from IPS fellow Paul Jacobs, who declared "I am for the defeat of the United States in Vietnam". IPS provided essential support for Philip Agee, who exposed Western intelligence agents to the Soviets -- he announced "I aspire to be a Communist revolutionary." Congress people Dan Edwards (D. CA), John Conyers (D.Mich) Pat Schroeder (D.Colo.) and C. Schumer (D.N.Y.) voted against the Intelligence Agents Identities Protection Act, designed to prevent Philip Agee types from publishing names of intelligence sources and imperiling lives. IPS visiting fellow Elizabeth Becker wrote stories for the *Washington Post* belittling the Cambodian holocaust, tacitly supporting Pol Pot and attacking Lon Nol, the anti-Communist Cambodian leader.

Orlando Letelier was an agent of influence for Cuban Intelligence (DGI) and Chilean Communists organized in East Germany. Senator Frank Church (D.Id.) headed the Church Senate Intelligence Committee in attacks on Defense Department policies in Vietnam; he filled key positions on advice of Letelier and Barnet. Evidence of Letelier's Communists connections were found in his briefcase when as an IPS/TNI director his car was shattered by a bomb. Letelier had ongoing relations with 24 leading reporters and editors in the major media, many with the *Times* and *Post* who kept his East German connections out of the "mainstream". *Post's* Karen de Young, described him as a "tall, charming redhead who lived quietly in the Maryland suburbs". Love of the media for Communism still shines.

IPS also had a powerful influence in U.S. church hierarchy, with a controlling influence in New York's Riverside Church through Cora Weiss, daughter of Communist Sam Rubin and wife of IPS chairman Peter Weiss. The *Sojourners* was founded in 1976 and was soon under IPS influence. Rev. Billy Graham gave *Sojourners* an interview in 1979. A few years later Graham was invited to Moscow where he found "religious freedom", in another great Kremlin propaganda coup. Cora Weiss was just one of a whole organization of people who belonged to no church, but had long promoted an ideology implacably hostile to humanness and freedom, to religion itself, and who were given influential positions in the heart of America's religious institutions.

Those who are skeptical of the reality of conspiracies should examine how often conspiracies have been continued even long after they have been disavowed. (See Refs. 14 and 16.) Attacks were made on IPS, particularly by Rael Jean Isaac in *Jewish Week* and *Mainstream*, noting IPS monopolization of *New York Times* op-ed, on October 1, 2, 15, 26, 28 and November 13, 1979. She noted that IPS, "a veritable hive of anti-Israeli activity", "consistently advocated policies in accord with the Soviets." But this was post-Vietnam; we must return to the roots of that tragedy.

Secretaries of State and War, Hull and Stimson, were "horrified" at what became known as the Morgenthau Plan, which came out of FDR's 1944 Quebec Conference for the "pastoralization" of Germany. Stimson was appalled at the idea of turning Central Europe, the most advanced continent in the world, into a "ghost territory", "a gift of nature into a dirt heap". "Stupefaction" was Hull's word. Churchill was violently opposed, and went along only to get the six and one half billion dollars FDR offered for his acquiescence; Hull so admitted in his *Memoirs*. The diabolical Plan had come from Stalin to Harry Dexter White, to Morgenthau. Though denied, it was never, never slackened from Dresden to the confiscation of whole German factories, almost whole companies. No voice was raised against it in the media, nor in churches; Truman was forced to end it only as the Berlin Blockade began. It was what Roosevelt and Stalin wanted. So it would be with "Get Diem" in Vietnam.

John Kenneth Galbraith, a backer of the Liberal Project, stopped off for a three day, first visit in Saigon, on returning home for the holidays near the end of 1961 from his Ambassadorship to India where Kennedy had marooned him. The old Harvard jungle fighter could see that President Ngo Dinh Diem was the central support of anti-Communism and order in South Vietnam, and if anti-Communism was bad in Washington it certainly was so in Saigon. "Diem is exceedingly bad . . . only solution is to drop Diem . . . neither difficult nor dangerous", he cabled to Kennedy.(17)

This became the fixed policy in Washington and the media, never altering until Diem was dead. It flew in the face of an evaluation of Diem by liberal Justice W.O. Douglas: "a hero . . . revered . . . honest and independent and stood firm;"(18) and by historian Joseph Buttinger, whose history of Vietnam, *The Small Dragon* (1958) acclaimed Diem's rebuilding as the "miracle of Vietnam".(19) Every one of Kennedy's top advisers, in State, Defense, CIA, and Vice President, were adamantly against removing Diem; no one could take his place, chaos would result, the war effort would be set back indefinitely. In 1963 South Vietnam was the sole exporter of rice in southeast Asia, exporting 300,000 tons; after the assassination of the government, increasing chaos made importing rice necessary.

It was known in Washington that Ho Chi Minh had in the summer of 1963 openly broached settlement talks with Diem, so the coup had to be hurried lest they "sign a peace and kick us out". At a National Security Council meeting just three days before the coup, Kennedy had to be informed that the whole governmental structure in the South would collapse, because the Vietnamese coup group would never accept Diem's province and village chiefs. And Bobby noted the madness of "supporting a coup . . . for a man not known to us".(20)

Had there been the slightest interest in "getting out", now was an ideal time; but not with the government destroyed. The "Diem must go" to move the war along U.S. coup-group of second and third stringers, met in the Oval Office with Kennedy at 11 a.m., July 4, 1963, with everyone else out of town. Under Secretaries of State Geo. Ball and Ave. Harriman, Assistant Secretary Roger Hilsman, National Security Adviser, McGeorge Bundy and his assistant Michael Forrestal(21). These were the renegades, associates of Marcus Raskin (a former Bundy aide) and Richard Barnet (of Arms Control) who had resigned to form the KGB outpost known as IPS, leaving behind particularly Harriman and Hilsman, to take care of Diem. Henry Cabot Lodge, Kennedy's new proconsul in Saigon would drive the coup.

David Halberstam had been sent to Saigon by the *New York Times* for the same reason that Herb Matthews had been sent to Havana a few years earlier, to undermine a non-Communist government. Halberstam, Neil Sheehan from U.P., Mert Perry of *Time*, and Viet Communist Pham Xuan An,(22) would shape public opinion, with Hanoi trained bonzi Tri Quang providing the street theater: riots, immolations, and destruction. Harriman had provided for the Harriman-Ho Highway (Ho Chi Minh Trail) with his neutralization of Laos which Diem desperately fought, knowing that the North would use Laos as a neutral conduit for moving troops and supplies south, eventually to within 50 miles of Saigon. All of this while Kennedy titillated Senate wives.

In the struggle for and against the coup, the (pro-Communist) coup group became fanatical. Harriman once yanked out his hearing aid, another time refused Kennedy's Ambassador to Saigon, Fred Nolting, a ride in "his" limousine back to State after a meeting. Edward R. Murrow wrote "Feelings ran so high . . . that the process of reason could not function"(23); for Hilsman, "facts became irrelevant"; AP's Malcolm Brown was told to take a month off to cool down. Years later Hilsman admitted "We had not the knowledge necessary to do what we were trying to do" (to "New Frontier" the Viets during a savage war). Supporters of Communism or liberalism always win over intimidated oppositions by becoming sufficiently enraged.

The coup group received Kennedy's unconsidered consent to a coup-order telegram which was sent to Saigon August 24, 1963. Lodge, the new proconsul in charge, cabled back, "in full agreement with policy . . . instructed to carry out". Years later he bleated, "they were asking me to overthrow a government I hadn't even presented my credentials to." The fact is that he met with the Communists first. In Sept., 1963, Lodge referred to it as a "command decision". Shortly after Lodge arrived, Diem assented to his generals' request to go after Tri Quang, the Hanoi agent impersonating a Buddhist bonzi (monk); Tri Quang escaped and Lodge gave him sanctuary in the American embassy until after the Diem assassinations.

Geo. Ball asked Nolting, the Ambassador whom Lodge replaced, "What would happen if there was a coup?" Nolting told him "feuding factions would create such disruptions that the country might be lost to the Communists". Ball was one of the original coup group which pushed forward, though fought by the military, CIA, and Lyndon Johnson. A decade later, E.M. Yoder in reviewing Ball's book *Another Pattern*, gushed, "Most revealing glimpse of Ball's virtue, (is) his lonely effort to head off U.S. Viet involvement". This is too fatuous to be ignorance. Destroying the government was the surest way to tie Uncle Sam's tail to an interminable disaster. Don't think this was not understood by the renegades. Johnson warned them, but was left holding the bag — his options, a "build-up" or a Dunkirk.

News of the assassinations came when Kennedy was in a meeting; General Taylor wrote, he "saw a look of shock and dismay . . . I had never seen before. Kennedy rushed from the room". Later when told the Ngos were tyrants, Kennedy insisted, "No! They did the best they could for their country".(24) Four months after the murdering of the Diem government, McNamara reported back to Johnson (in *Pentagon Papers*), "Control structure from Saigon down into hamlets has disappeared".(25) He and Gen. Taylor had reported in Oct., 1963, "the military campaign making great progress"; the South exported 300,000 tons of rice. By 1965 it would import rice.

A few months before Jack's last trip to Dallas, Bobby had proudly announced, "We are going to stay in Vietnam until we win!" A few years later after serving most of that time as chief officer of Justice in the government, Bobby Kennedy orated before a howling mob, "We are doing in Vietnam . . . what Hitler did to the Jews!"

Note that he clearly distanced himself form the "We" which he likened to Hitler. Why ? or how? Power. Bobby

101

recognized that the media had already spoken, and a vile corruption was in control. As Red Cronkite would put it, "the media would decide what was news", and truth. Bobby now saw that the power was no longer with the "We" of America. It soon became the media's claim that the "We" of America was responsible for the evil Viet War, and the "best and brightest" vanished in the wings. Government would be of, by, and for the media. The "silent majority" might speak once more, in the 1972 election; not after that.

Immediately after the JFK assassination in Dallas by Lee Harvey Oswald, a recognized Communist with connections in Cuba, Mexico, and Moscow, the U.S. Office of Information declared Dallas to be the "center of conservatism". Soviet spokesmen took their cue in turn, asserting categorically, "a rightist plot was responsible". This was silly, as irrational as blaming Nixon for John Dean's caper in Watergate. *Cui Bono* !

The Warren Commission's conclusion that the assassination of "Camelot" had been "the result of hatred and bitterness . . . injected into the nation's life by bigots", was fatuous when released. In spite of Oswald's known Communist connections he was nevertheless declared a "lone wolf", there was no conspiracy, even as the attack on a conservative conspiracy continued. An excellent account of Kennedy and his death has been written by Christopher Lasch.(26)

"Dark forces of hatred and evil . . . will not simply kill and maim . . . they could destroy America," insisted a ranking member of the House Judiciary Committee in the wake of the great liberal justice Earl Warren's Commission. Warren and Roosevelt had been the screws who "interned" the "loyal Japanese-Americans," which the media made into the disgrace of the "We" of America.

It was necessary for the media to deny Oswald connections, in order to exonerate the KGB and Castro, or any leftist source -- accompanied by the convenient assassination of Oswald by a man who had spent time in Castro's headquarters. The entire nation was charged with "collective guilt" in James Reston's "A Portion of Guilt for All," in the *New York Times*.(27) "All" did not include, of course, the *Times;* it was the "We" of America. "Conspiracy!" charged the liberals. So what? The whole century has been a conspiracy.

Who would profit from the removal of Kennedy? To assert "dark forces of evil" or "the hatred and bitterness of bigots" as Justice Warren phrased it, was itself a bigoted calumny by those seeking to deceive and to hide the truth. In the world of liberal-left communism, with Vietnam and the recent explosion of chaos following the coup, did Kennedy with all his sordid weaknesses of character still have the ability to grab America's attention? Would he rise to the occasion and fill the void he had created in Vietnam? Or would forces deep within the media-academia regime, that had struggled so long and so hard to destroy Diem, choose not to wait to see?

What needs to be comprehended is that the fatuous slander of American "hatred and bitterness", (after the Fifties!?) is a blatant introduction to the charges that would be raised and chanted of "evil America", for the purpose of gaining a Communist victory in Vietnam.

The callow youths of the Sixties, tearing at social vestments of which they had no comprehension were not "idealists", they were self-emasculated puppets, jigging and chanting for a Communist victory over their own peers, under the direction of people like the Frankfurt School of Jewish Communists; Adorno, Marcuse, and of others such as Wilhelm Reich offering free sex, like Dionysus to the Bacchae of Euripides.

Renegade historians begin their story of the Viet War with the "Johnson buildup"; actually the rational war ended with destruction of the Viet government which Johnson had fought desperately to prevent. He was left with no option other than a Dunkirk withdrawal. After the Diem assassinations the Communist North began expanding guerilla infiltration of the South; under eight thousand in 1963 it went to over double that in 1964 and up to twenty times by 1968 (141,081 by Hanoi data). Johnson spent four years Americanizing the war, ending with 1968 Tet, in which the Communists shot their whole wad, suffered "staggering" damage requiring three years for recovery, but which New York media transformed into a vast U.S. defeat.

Among the many significant incidents that have undergone "liberal-cleansing" from the "mainstream", is President Johnson's 1966 request to the Jewish War Veterans Commander, Malcolm Tarlov: to explain to Jewish leaders that their increasing antiwar position could force abandonment of SEATO "commitments" in Vietnam, and hence "the less explicit commitments to Israel would be jeopardized" as well as U.S. support for Soviet Jewry. Professor Judith Klinghoffer of Rutgers University in a letter to *The New Republic* wrote that the "shocked Jewish leaders" were convinced that Johnson would "back down". But he refused. She goes on, Max Kampelman declared it "a warning shot to the Jewish community . . . " Actually little change followed. Bui Tin, a former colonel who served on the general staff of the North's Army, and later became the editor of the official Viet paper the *People's Daily*, gave an interview published in the *Wall Street Journal*(28). He quoted Ho Chi Minh, "We don't need to win . . . only hit them until they get out". Another Communist general bragged of "winning the war in the streets of New York".

After Johnson's Americanization and shattering of the North by Tet 1968, came Nixon's Vietnamization and withdrawal. The continuing major flaw in American operations in Vietnam, following the failure to implement an interdiction of the Ho Chi Minh Trail by Eisenhower and the terribly renegade neutralization of Laos by Kennedy-Harriman, was the media's insistence that Cambodia was a "sanctuary", for the Communist supply line.

Cambodia's Sihanouk had urged the Johnson

administration in 1968 to use "hot pursuit (of Communist forces) in uninhabitable areas" (taken over by Communist armies); it would be "liberating us".(29) *But* it must be kept a secret; Big Brother (China) is just across the border. Various strikes into Cambodia were made without protest from any quarter; they in fact hurried the peace talks which had started in Paris, so claimed the *New York Times.*

During WW II when we were fighting *for* Communism, no journalist would have considered releasing secret information, no matter how received. When we were fighting *against* Communism in 1970, revealing leaked or stolen security information and exposing the "evils of America" became major media objectives. The "secret" Cambodian bombings were to protect American troops from sudden Communist thrusts from the "sanctuaries." The fact of the air strikes was leaked to the press and media, and liberal-Communist "outrage" reached a 10 level. "Military Hallucination" stormed the *Times*. When Congress was considering Nixon's impeachment, discarding one charge after another as unsupportable, a Senator arose, perhaps Frank Church, and demanded "What about the bombing of Cambodia?" Victory for the Communists in Vietnam was the basis for the whole turmoil of Watergate.

Communists inspired and led SDS violence, particularly their riots at Kent State in Ohio, had increased in destructiveness since 1968. A black renegade newspaper at Kent State had urged "killing of all racists", "killing policemen". A 1969 SDS "Spring Offensive" led to 58 arrests and the revocation of their charter; a threat was made to burn down the whole campus. Bernadine Dohrn, of the grisly Tate murders, was a frequent speaker. Jerry Rubin urged "kill your parents", Jesse Jackson demanded "topple the system". The rioters' faculty adviser was Dr. Sidney Johnson, a Communist Party member since 1936 and eulogized by the *Daily Worker* a few years later on his death.(30)

The rioter's attention was turned to the Cambodia

bombings, and on May 1, 1970, a thousand rioters gathered; on May 2, two thousand "students" tried to burn the ROTC building, and attacked police and firemen who worked to contain it; a small National Guard contingent arrived. Rocks were thrown, golf balls with nails punched through them and pieces of glass were hurled at police and Guardsmen. Ten blacks stalked past the Guardsmen spitting on them. Bags of feces were thrown at them. A grand jury later noted "A level of obscenity and vulgarity never before witnessed".

On May 4 massed "students" attacked the Guards. Tear gas canisters were quickly thrown back at them; so they were now wearing masks. The Guards retreated up a hill away from a parking lot and sports field. Suddenly they wheeled and fired without removing masks. Most shots went not near them but down in the parking lot below; 28 Guardsmen fired 55 M-1 rounds in 13 seconds.(31) Soon a thousand more "students" gathered for an attack, but were deterred. The school was closed. Such were the "idealists", for whom a whole flood of alligator tears has been shed.

Nixon as President succeeded in bringing home over a half million young men who had been sent into a jungle hellhole and abandoned by Congress. He made a world astounding peace agreement with the Chinese leaders, and forced the North Vietnamese into a peace treaty which prohibited further Communist supplying or infiltration, and guaranteed U.S. continued help to the South which by 1973 was holding its own. A viable peace had resulted, the negotiators receiving Nobel Peace Prizes.

Impeachment of Nixon talk had started not long after he was inaugurated in 1969; they increased in vehemence right into the 1972 campaign. When Nixon, never a "popular" personality, won by an unprecedented landslide, the media and the "peace" renegades rose in wrath. "We must see that nothing like this is attempted again".(32) Allegedly the *Post's* Ben Bradlee.

That no attempt was made to separate Nixon's

interests from the nation's national security interests evinces that they were in fact in agreement, and that the "impeachment" was principally to destroy Nixon's Vietnam success. A Democratic member of the impeachment committee (Judiciary Committee) was appalled, "If these meetings were televised the country would impeach us". The *Village Voice* reported how reporters snickered at Presidential defenders; "how slovenly and vague" were the Committee's articles of impeachment; "how little real investigation", how "suppositional and circumstantial". In the final article of impeachment the heart of the matter was the President's policy of obstruction of justice and interference with the investigation. But the Committee could not, did not, say when, how, or in what respect, nor how the President had declared that policy.

Since the American press had become most irrational in their hatred of Nixon, look at foreign comments by people with no visible ax to grind. France's leading newspaper declared "none of the points (for impeachment) . . . backed by facts. They are denying the most elementary right of an accused man, to know precisely for what . . . to defend himself". The London *Daily Express* called it "Political Peyton Place", the *Daily Mail* saw a "lynch-mob behavior." Veteran journalist Richard Wilson noted that "The tone of the attack" seeks to present Nixon's offenses as "so enormous they threatened the government. When the chief offense (the break in) of the Bill of Impeachment grew from a ludicrous act of which Nixon knew nothing."

Watergate was the culmination of a decade long struggle by the liberal regime to bring a Communist victory in Vietnam. From robotic idiots chanting for a Communist victory over their own peers, to raucous media demands that Communist "sanctuaries" be honored, and on to treasonous "leaking" of wartime security information, the message was that "America needed its nose bloodied".

The Watergate break-in had nothing to do with the war or with politics; but through it "an American president was toppled by the world's oldest profession."(33) John Dean had assumed a leading role in the "plumbers", or leak detectors, made necessary by the liberal media's massive efforts to sabotage the Viet War by releasing national security information, without which there would have been no Watergate. Dean's girl friend, and wife-to-be, was listed in a black-book of call-girls for visiting Demo big-wigs, and he had determined that that black-book was in a particular desk in Democratic headquarters. He obtained a key to the desk and organized a plumber's break-in to retrieve the book. When they were caught, Dean explained he was looking for Democratic dirt for Nixon.

It is "A cruel hoax to pretend that the most powerful institutions of the media did not have the wherewithal to uncover the story, not to mention the historians and writers . . . the results . . . a version of a *treason of the clerks*."(34) Renata Adler, one of the "inner seven" who worked on John Doar's impeachment inquiry staff wrote, "It has always been an anomaly that whatever we know about the offenses that led to Nixon's departure is based on what was known to John Dean". "There was never any doubt among Doar and his group that unless there was overwhelming evidence of Nixon's *innocence* (e.a.) . . . the President must be impeached." "In light of the Church Committee report and other documents . . . the records of the impeachment inquiry would support a claim that Nixon was hounded from office, and the impeachment inquiry was just another phase of the cover-up."(35)

It is a cheap calumny on the American people to say that they "tired of Vietnam." They gave to Nixon, never a popular figure in the media, a nearly unprecedented victory for ending the war with a peace treaty, bringing home over half a million young men and making peace with China. And these were accomplished against the vehement, even violent, opposition of the entire liberals world, including many of the churches, under the nearly direct guidance of Communist partisans.

The so-called "Nixon crimes" were distortions of Nixon's attempts to ward off attacks, from media, from radicals, and even from within government. The reality of the evil of Vietnam and Watergate -- there would have been no Watergate without Vietnam -- is that the predominate forces within America came under the control of people and groups seeking a Communist victory. Watergate was but an excuse, as was the "Cambodian bombing", for attacking the national forces seeking an honorable withdrawal from Vietnam. What was wanted was a Communist "victory" ("in the streets of New York"), and a humiliation and a stigmatizing of America as evil. So Tri Quang had told Marguerite Higgins nearly a decade earlier. The tragic evil of the Viet War cannot be fully comprehended without reading her book(36).

"The ultimate price of the (anti-Nixon) coup was to defraud a nation of its past". Its purpose was "to maintain a prescribed course for America", as laid down by Franklin Roosevelt at Yalta. And so "Reputations and fortunes were made (and destroyed). Books and movies were confected. A generation of students stood inspired . . . by a fraud."(37)

Fraudulence, however, was just entering the big-time "mainstream". Giant, prison muscled, multiple felon, Rodney King, in March of 1991 led police on a mad 100 mph-plus race, through many stop-lights and signs, endangering untold lives and property. Stopped by a heavy chain in a dangerous area, his threats led a highway patrol to pull a gun on him; he could have been shot. Los Angeles police arrived, ordered guns away, but they too were jeered. King threw off a "swarm" of four officers like puppy dogs. Tasered twice, he rose from the second in a vicious attack on police; it was shoot or use sticks. He was brought under control in just over a minute, with only "minor lacerations" and drugs on his medical report.

Many lawyers watched the trial, not of King but of the arresting officers. There was no miscarriage of justice, Arthur Miller, Harvard professor and ABC legal commentator and thereby partial to the media, so declared on "Good Morning

America".(4,30,93). "The verdict was not outrageous . . . (I) might have come to the conclusion that the officers used reasonable force . . . (King) never submitted". "Like it not, that is what the video shows . . . I have never felt so hesitant to say what I believe . . . I'm terrified of quotations out of context . . ." wrote lawyer Roger Parloff in the *American Lawyer*.(38) Fear again!

If Miller and Parloff knew that, then so did black L.A. Mayor Bradley and Sam Donaldson, and the black community. And there was nearly a week long interval between the end of the trial and the public announcement of the not-guilty verdict, during which time Bradley, Sam, and all the others, had an inviolable duty to declare that truth in order to dampen the growing enthusiasm for a riot. The media had other visions. "A motorist . . . beaten into insensitivity", Sam Donaldson; "nearly to death", Wm. Raspberry; "to a pulp", John Chancellor. When the verdict came even the mayor incited to riot, and the media led the way. But it was not a riot, and it was not the black community. It was criminal gangs that looted for three days, unhindered.

Hugh Hewitt, lawyer and L.A. TV host: "(TV coverage) encouraged opportunistic criminals." *Newsweek*: "TV told them where to go". Harry Schwartz of *NY Times* editorial board: "The tragedy . . . was the direct result of irresponsibility of the media . . . TV convicted the police months before the trial began."(39) Tom Sowell: "58 percent of blacks characterized the riots as totally unjustified". Wm. Safire of *NY Times*: "The bulwark of civil liberty is the jury system; the Am. Civil Liberties Union abandoned principle by failing to defend the rights of jurors to be free of threats of punishment by publicity".(40) Paula Zahn of CBS demanded to know from a juror why they "hadn't ever considered the impact of the verdict on the public"; as if our legal system was following the Soviets in featuring "show trials".(41) Lester Alan Horvitz asserted that "California courts had failed to win a conviction" in the Rodney King case, as though conviction was the purpose, like

Vyshinsky's purge courts. Such statements, here and throughout liberalism, are voluntary expression of its malignant (as evil nature) treason, as betrayal of a sacred trust.

Readers will understand that the intent here is not to rehabilitate, nor to amend the injustices done to the victims of FDR's persecutions, of anti-McCarthyism, or Nixon, or any of the others. The central purpose is to bring to the American people the reality of the evil of the liberal regime that controls all public opinions, education, and the awarding of calumny or honor, and that works assiduously to denigrate the people of America in order to facilitate their grab for total power.

IX HATRED AND TRUTH

The tension between hatred and truth which has increasingly marked the flow of modern events is inherent in the deceptions arising from Machiavellian promises. The Enlightener's hatred for religion -- Voltaire's "Ecrasez L'Infame!" -- and for Jews especially, was passed on to their socialist offspring, and created modern anti-Semitism. Marx by 1840s had come to realize that the promises of ideal socialism were worthless; his transition to the teaching of class hatred and hard Communism, Lenin claimed, was marked by the publication of his rabidly anti-Semitic essay, "On the Jewish Question". "What intellectuals have done repeatedly in various countries and centuries is to get people to hate one another, fight one another, tear the social fabric that makes humanness possible", wrote Tom Sowell. "Hatred . . . is aimed downward, at the public at large . . . the intellectual elite loathes the nation it rules,".(1) Nietzsche pointed to intellectuals, not Yahoos, as the most vicious haters.

Sowell referred to "taught hatred", as opposed to true hatred, which is no more outlawable than is hunger. People may say they hate broccoli or their neighbors when it is but dislike or contempt. Contempt is proper for indecencies or violations within a society; true hatred can be justified only for external attacks upon children, family, society, upon survival! It is taught hatred that is in tension with truth, as is well exemplified in the case of religion, for which so many people voice a vehement hatred, without even knowing what it is -- similarly for capitalism.

True hatred is based on fear, as love is based on need. Nearly everything people do is urged by some innate need, but what we do in response must be reasoned from a culture with a human purpose, in terms of a perceived reality. Reason's imagination is the source of man's genius when in the service of a human purpose; but is the generator of all of man's evil, including taught hatred, in serving an inhuman purpose.

Franklin Roosevelt had sacrificed the lives of thousands of young men, coldly and deliberately, to gain entry to a war whose principal result was the empowerment of Communism around the world. It was after that horror that the Manichaean split between the American people and the collectivist regime, announced by Lippmann in 1936, became undeniable. Lillian Hellman, defended Stalin's bloody purges and his pact with Hitler; her *Scoundrel Time* attacked those who objected to the glorification of the Soviets in Hollywood, as in "Mission To Moscow". Hollywood's Communist partisans drove out Budd Schulberg, Elia Kazan and many others; Frances Farmer was driven to the madhouse. Read for yourself much of the truth of Hellman's "fiction", the Hollywood Ten's Dmytryk's admission of "complicity in a terrible hoax", of Communist Harry Bridges' escapes, and much more in *The New Republic*.(2)

Yet on Oct. 27, 1997, the Motion Picture Academy audience reacted with *stormy applause* as prominent actors (Billy Crystal and Kevin Spacey) celebrated the Communist "Hollywood Ten as heroes and defenders of freedom!" Who says that Communism is dead? *The Nation's* Victor Navasky had written "every one (was) . . . deeply involved in Communism . . . were zealots for Communism, not Constitutional rights". Former editor of pinkish *PM*, Arnold Beichman declared, "You never forget how otherwise intelligent people will lie with a straight face to safeguard the image of Communism".

Thus we see the eternal struggle between taught hatred and truth. Such hatred is conquered not by more hatred but by truth. Leftist liberal Edmund Wilson, famous for *To The Finland Station*, finally denounced Communism as "One of the most hideous tyrannies the world has ever known". Hitler could never have come to power, nor would there have been a Holocaust without the threat of Communism, often led by Jews; read centrist historian Paul Johnson's *Modern Times*.(3)

"Hatred is our greatest problem . . . " has frequently been declared, even by former President Clinton. Alec Baldwin arose in a meeting protesting Impeachment and shouted, "We should all go to Washington and stone Henry Hyde to death, and then go to their homes and kill their wives and children. We would kill their families . . ."(4) "I'd like to see someone blow up one of their churches . . . spit on them . . . kick them in the head," editorialized Michelle Goldberg in the SUNY student newspaper, concerning the vandalizing of an approved Christian display. Noam Chomsky was bowed and scraped-to by the media while he was spouting "the evil of America, as an article of faith". But when he suggested that the Holocaust might be a "Zionist hoax", he discovered what Tom Wolfe meant by "the most intense vilification you can imagine".

Taught hatred produces the worst social violence. Mass hatred was urged by the abolitionists, as learned from socialists before the Civil War. It burst into flame against anti-Communism in the Fifties, became a wild-fire against evil America in the Sixties and has become central to the regime's ravaging of our human society. When America went to war to defeat Nazism and to end the idea that the State should tell people what to think; "gun control, abortion, homosexuality, non-white immigration," were all considered pernicious to free society, and "as destructive as Nazism, or Communism". Now *opposition to them* is perceived in the mainstream to be as Nazism itself.

If the notion of hate-speech forces legalized censorship of language in the public square, then it must be made to apply to hatred of religion and civilization which are far more critical classifications than race and class.

Harry Stein, "former" writer for NY *Times* and *Playboy*, told of suggesting at a dinner party, "Quayle may have had a point" about Murphy Brown's unfathered child. A friend turned red, "literally sputtered, 'Jesus Christ, when did you become a fascist?'", i.e., anti-Semite.(5) A noted *Wall Street*

Journal writer charged that mere accusations alone of "racism, homophobia, anti-Semitism, or fascism," are sufficient to destroy a person, as Harry Stein and dozens others have experienced. "The push for hate crimes is designed to produce negative stereotypes about normal middle-class Americans." J. Rubenstein's recent *New York Times* review of Lee's, *The Beast Awakens* (America, that is), announced, "Neo-Nazis and the religious right see eye-to-eye". Abe Foxman of the Anti-Defamation League warned that "the religious right brings a rhetoric of suspicion, fear, and hatred". If that is "anti-defamation" what would pro-defamation be?

Mr. Rubenstein quite properly recognized that the "religious right" is in fact the only significant organized force set on opposing a destruction of human society by his brand of fascism. "Look . . . They're Yahoos, rednecks and racists . . . and we're not. That's the difference", declared a prominent New York rabbi.(6)

An educational conference to support the homosexual program, keynoted by Democratic Congressman Lewis from Georgia, attacked Christianity and urged "forcing schools to adopt homosexual policies" and plans for keeping the media from giving straight people any coverage. "The fear of the Religious Right is that the schools of today are the government of tomorrow. And you know they're right", Deanna Duby of the National Education Association, told the conference.(7)

Nobel economist James Buchanan has recently explained "the viability of free society" depends upon the existence of "an animating principle . . . a soul . . . a moving spirit for constructive change". The Greeks sought "a dominating ideal", "an absolute authority" that arose from "something in man that is divine . . . " Buchanan noted that President Reagan "tapped into *the City on a Hill* of the Puritans, that deeply resonated in America". However, "We have failed to save the soul of liberalism", as an animating principle, concluded Buchanan.(8)

Professor Buchanan misunderstands, liberalism never had a soul; liberalism evolved when society was a concept so deeply embedded in the human consciousness that its absence was unimaginable. And liberalism-socialism arose as little more than an economic scheme overlaying a human society, even on Christianity as Comte would have it. However Marx and others became aware that it would never work; liberalism (or idealistic socialism) was but a parasite, feeding on the decaying trunk of a fallen order unable to support one of its own.

Normal men will fight and die for their human society, their family, their home and way of living, and can truly hate only their attackers. The greatest contribution of the Greeks to humanity was the evolution of a social purpose for maintaining rational social guidance for a society without which progress becomes impossible, and a body of knowledge, a culture, for guidance in that purpose. This is generally unrecognized, as is a great contribution of Christianity: the addition of an organized body of workers, dedicated to explicating, exemplifying and celebrating the social purpose in a culture. Previous support groups were either so limited as to be essentially different in kind, or were the priesthoods for the god-king empires, and servants not of society but of power.

The French writer Julien Benda in his *Treason of the Clerks*, explained that every human society required a body of workers: teachers, writers, organizers, and thinkers, dedicated to attending the needs of society and especially of its soul; hence the treason when they acted to destroy society. Tocqueville warned long ago that if the people allowed the State all initiatory power they would gradually slide into a sub human servitude, and *we can see it*! Without an organized society there will be no force to guard freedom, to promote progress and humanness. When in 1967 the German student radical Rudi Duetschke was asked how he could expect to press Communism on free people, he replied confidently, "By going through the institutions".(9) This was the strategy used by the network of socialist cells of John Dewey, Morris Cohen, and others, as the last century was beginning and later credited to the Marxist Gramsci. Socialists and their liberal helpers had to operate more subversively in American than in Europe, so much so that almost until the Sixties, liberals dissembled a "wonder" at the absence of a socialist movement in America.

This was nonsense, certainly after Walter Lippmann in 1936 announced that collectivists had already taken over. During WW II Franklin Roosevelt quite openly used vast quantities of American blood and treasure for the most evil purpose of empowering Communism around the world, and became enraged when opposed, even at his Attorney General who hesitated to prosecute citizens for exercising the First Amendment rights in peace time. Later when liberals were opposed in their efforts to destroy the Viet government and eventually to bring a Communist victory, their rage struck at the stability of our nation; our own victory was abandoned and the Paris Peace Accord abrogated. Then came the shameful trial and imprisonment of the Rodney King arresting officers, and "real hate for America" by Bryant Gumbel.

More destructive was the media's playing the L.A. Loot as an "uprising" of the black community, when actually 58 percent of blacks characterized it as "totally unjustified". It is bad enough when polarization exists; it is criminal when the media depicts hoodlums and looters as justified and as representing the black community. Police officers who had put their lives on the line to bring in a dangerous felon, with only minor lacerations, were declared by the media to be "animals" and long prison sentences were sought. On the other hand black thugs who took the head of a passerby in their hands and mushed it with a chunk of cement were "victims of society" and essentially let off.

And the terrible evil is that no one dares to call the defenders of these criminals *renegades*. People whine and proclaim "evil America", like Abigail Van Buren, *"our everlasting shame for putting 100,000 loyal American in concentration camps."* more pernicious than ignorance or credulity can excuse. They were not in concentration camps nor interned, as were the Japanese ethnics in Canada who were not released until 1948.

If there was any shame or crime concerning the Japanese it falls on those famous lovers of goodness and mercy, Franklin Roosevelt and Prosecutor Earl Warren. It was FDR who produced the "day of infamy" and Warren who insisted on ousting the Japs from the War Department's designated "defense districts" in California. Once ejected, some place had to be provided for them, for most could find neither jobs nor a place to sleep. Some 10,000 did find a place on their own and were never bothered further. Relocation camps had to be built for the others; thousands left the camps for jobs with the Army's help, and up to 4300 young people left each year to attend colleges. Relocation centers provided better schools, better food, and better medical care than available to tens of thousands of war workers, such as those at Willow Run. The American people sent them books, arts and crafts materials, sports equipment, musical instruments and even graduation robes. They were given $21 a month as were Army draftees, and everything, even movies, were provided.(10)

And what about the "loyal Japanese-Americans"? They had lived in ethnic colonies where eternal loyalty to the Emperor was enforced; all were expected to prepare the way for his troops, and those who failed were to be shot. Over 3000 were immediately charged with treason when war did come. It is necessary to note that Magic intercepts and FBI surveillance had long identified them, but FDR left them undisturbed lest it queer the Jap attack he was promoting. Some 20,000 demanded repatriation *during war time*, and not a single one reported on treason. These things have long been well known and for writers to continue to harp on the "interment" of "loyal Americans", even the Chief Justice of the Supreme Court, is shameful ignorance or deceit.(11)

There have been many assaults on Western civilization and humanness since Machiavelli's demonic dream, but most of them were accompanied with promises of something better. More recently the regime has gone out picking fights, with those who doubt its intentions or legitimacy. The Jewish Anti-Defamation League (ADL) has become a major source for identifying enemies of the regime, as noted in FDR's Great Sedition Trial. Michael Fitzpatrick, a part-time Jewish Defense League informant and convicted bomber, was used by the FBI in an attempt to entrap Malcolm X's daughter into giving evidence that Louis Farrahkan was involved in her father's (Malcolm's) murder.(12) Then came the hatred for "black church burnings" in the South.

"Flames of Hate", headlined the NY *Daily News*; "can be traced to an environment of bigotry and hatred", from NY *Times*; "Echos of Bigotry" reported *USA Today*; "the conspiracy of racism itself" charged Al Gore, "a white riot" added Jesse Jackson. Hillary Clinton compared the church burnings to (gasp) "The Holocaust!" Then AP reported two-thirds were white churches. The *New Yorker* reported burning as "lowest in fifteen years". Not a racist epidemic, but "a deliberate hoax", wrote Michael Fumento in *Wall Street Journal* and *Commentary*.(13) It was all for money; the Center for Democratic Review (CDR), a Marxist group as is the National Council of Churches (NCC), shared a $7M take with Wm. Kunstler's Center for Constitutional Rights. Clinton threw in $10M from the taxpayers, after remembering "vivid and painful" childhood memories -- the Arkansas *Demo-Gazette* reported not a single church burned in 1958 or the 60s in Arkansas. NCC took in $100,000 per day, teaching hatred for America.

In 1989 Bureau of Alcohol, Tobacco, and Firearms (BATF) agents succeeded with a big bribe in pressuring indigent Randy Weaver of Ruby Ridge, Idaho, into sawing-off two shotguns, even against his admonition that it was illegal. Then it was "Gotcha!" Tell us about the white supremacists out here. He refused and was harassed until early 1991. Then an 18 month period of intense surveillance and harassment ensued, with military aerial reconnaissance producing photos studied by the military; psychological profiles were paid for; $130,000 worth of solar-powered long-range spy cameras, and mail was intercepted. They even had the menstrual cycle of Weaver's teen age daughter determined, and a "scenario" planned around it.(14) All for a minor entrapment?

It is not clear who smelled out the orthodoxy of the media-labeled "white supremacists" in the barren foothills of northern Idaho, so insignificant, so unknown, as to require such effort to locate, or why they needed looking into more than did Communist groups (denied to the FBI in 1972), or the "Black Panthers". Common sense points to ADL. Suspected ADL agents were caught red-handed with over "10,000 individual dossiers" obtained by an illegal, gigantic domestic spying operation in San Francisco in 1993. The Prosecutor planned serious charges, until mysteriously all charges were dropped and for a $75,000 "donation" the illegal dossiers were actually returned to ADL.

On August 21, 1992, six heavily armed, camouflaged U.S. Marshals sneaked onto Weaver's property and shot a dog. Another shot broke an arm of 14 year old Sammy Weaver who came out to call his dog. He was then shot in the back when running back to the cabin with one arm flopping. Kevin Harris returned fire killing a marshal who had gotten off seven previous shots. A federal appeals court concluded that Marshal Cooper shot and killed the boy after effectively disarming him.(15)

Compare the ready acquiescence in this overtly premeditated murder of an innocent boy, at his home and in view of his parents, by media, churches, social activists, and Justice Department officials, with the massive hubbub, hateful racist vituperations, and even a trampling down of Constitutional guarantees, over a few "superficial lacerations" received by multiple-felon, Rodney King, for brazenly and viciously attacking arresting officers, who could have with justification shot him. And these racist hypocrites vilify the Germans.

FBI assault troops were rushed in with orders to shoot any armed adult whether threatening or not. Four hundred agents swarmed over the foothills with automatic weapons, snipers, night-vision scopes, and black helicopters. And just as later at Waco, no attempt at all was made to negotiate a settlement for a minor and questionable offense. On August 23rd, Randy Weaver was shot in the back by one Ron Horiuchi as he opened the door to a shed where his son's corpse lay. Struggling to get back to the cabin, his wife, Vicki, standing on the stoop of their pitiful plywood shack with her 10 month old baby in her arms, tried to help him. Her face was blown away by a Horiuchi bullet. Marshal Service Director, Eduardo Gonzalez commended the men for "their exceptional courage and sound judgment", even as a Justice Department task force, including FBI officials, recommended criminal prosecutions.(16) Then for eight days, while the dead woman's body lay in the cabin, the agents taunted the family with loud speakers. "Good morning, Mrs. Weaver. We had pancakes for breakfast, did you?"(17) An obligatory grand jury and universal Christian condemnation never appeared.

Weaver was a Vietnam Green Beret, as was Bo Gritz who negotiated a surrender 11 days after the shootings. Gritz believed Vicki was shot purposely; the FBI profile said, ". . . if you get a chance, take Vicki Weaver out."(18) Weaver's pitiful one-room plywood cabin, lacking all modern conveniences and even a basement was repeatedly described by the attackers as a "fortress".

The government reports were full of lies, from FBI Director Freeh down. Freeh justified the shooting of the Weavers because "one of the suspects (wounded Randy struggling back to the cabin and Vicki with a baby in her arms) raised a weapon in the direction of a helicopter overhead". The Marshal's director, Wayne Smith, testified that no helicopter was flying.(19) The agent in charge of the assault, Larry Potts, gave the order to "shoot without provocation", despite Justice Department findings it violated the Constitution. Janet Reno's promotion of Potts was denounced by *New York Times*, *Washington Post* and *Wall Street*

Journal, while FBI Director Freeh lavishly praised the agents.

An Idaho jury found Weaver innocent of almost all charges. Harris's shooting of the Marshal was ruled to be self defense. Sammy Weaver's last words, as he answered his father's orders to return to the house from trying to save his dog that the marshal had shot, were "I'm coming Dad!" Then he was shot in the back as he hurried to comply. Justice Department lawyers argued in federal court that the agents were completely immune from liability simply because they were federal lawmen, like the NKVD or Gestapo.(20) It has been condemned as "Nazi", to justify actions as being "orders", like Eichman. An investigation of BATF practices of a few years back showed that three-fourths of their assaults had been directed at people who were engaged in no criminal activity. And it was none other than the local, leftist Demo Congressman, John Dingle, who declared them to be "jack-booted fascist thugs", on the basis of a fat dossier of previous activities.(21)

When it was liberal-Communists, "black separatists" (Panthers), and violent peaceniks, who bombed, set fires, and assaulted government in mass attacks, the liberals went all out to defend their rights. The Supreme Court prohibited even keeping track of them. Modern anti-Semitism, Aryan superiority, and the mass teaching to hate were all initiated and developed by Marxist groups, yet decent Americans are terrorized and murdered on the basis of lies that would do Vyshinsky justice.

Now these same liberals seek to delegitimize and pugnaciously to go out of their way to attack any and all people or ideas they feel to be in conflict with their version of Statism with a family-less, Constitution-less, freedom-less, and human-less, ant-hill. There have been countless cases where these renegades, suspecting some ideas yet lacking overt actions to indict, have had such action "performed", for evidence. This strategy, approximately the case for Randy Weaver, was in fact charged by the Jewish defense lawyer, Henry Klein, in FDR's Sedition Trial, as noted previously.

The Mt. Carmel (Tex.) Davidian Seventh-Day Adventist's church and compound was investigated for nine-weeks in 1992 by the Texas Child Protective Services, and reported no evidence of child abuse. Children were found to be "healthy, and well-adjusted."(22) In the fall of 1992, the BATF conducted a brief investigation of firearms, and pointedly declined a personal invitation from leader Koresh to inspect their shop and inventory, declaring them "completely legal firearms". D. Kopel and P.H. Blackman, in *No More Wacos*, asked, "What then was the BATF doing?" BATF has kept that unclear, but it is known that preparations for a raid were well underway by December, 1992. A BATF memo written five days before the raid on Feb. 28, 1993, scripted as "Showtime", explained "this operation will generate national attention", and their public relations director Sharon Wheeler invited reporters to "cover a weapons raid on a 'cult'". A planned "dynamic entry" -- a military assault -- necessitated the help of the Army's Joint Task Force (JTF) for planning, and that required the invention of a drug (meth) lab, to trigger a drug-war exception to Posse Comitatus.(23) It is known that BATF became aware that they had totally lost surprise, thus making the assault suicidal for which a Treasury Department report excoriated ATF leaders.(24)

Thus it was that tractors, pulling two cattle trailers, roared up front at Mt. Carmel disgorging nearly 80 masked and heavily armed agents, running and opening the shooting by firing at Davidian dogs.(25) Koresh unarmed, opened the front door and shouted, "What do you want? Women and children are here!" Shortly thereafter full fire broke out.(26) Three agents, former Clinton bodyguards, broke into second floor windows and were shot for their pains. At the start a Harvard trained Davidian lawyer (well regarded in Waco) called 911, "There are 75 men . . . shooting at us . . . there are women and children here . . . call it off." In about an hour a cease fire was ordered. Four agents and David Koresh's father-in-law who stood by him in the opened foyer were killed with five others; Koresh was shot in the hand. Comment on a Justice Department report admitted, "An armed assault by 100 agents was an attack *independent* of who fired first . . . Law does not (require) attackers to fire first (for) self defense".(27)

The next day the FBI swat team took over. All telephone lines were cut but one, on which the FBI complained of "Bible babble", and pressure began to undermine negotiations. The first week of the "siege", 21 children came out and two elderly women, who were immediately cuffed, shackled, and charged with murder -- good for negotiations. Then 12 more "adults exited the fortress", in gestapo jargon; electricity was shut off. The grounds were bulldozed, of automobiles, go-carts, children's toys, propane tanks, any "obstacle". Night playing of loud music, then huge floodlights, loud Tibetan chants, screams of slaughtered rabbits designed to make sleep impossible.(28) Refusal to release a video of the disaster, implicates the entire liberal gang in this unbelievable evil, and they are just learning.

Two "adult males" had "snuck" out the renegades reported. Then flash-bang grenades were fired at anyone who came out, and rolls of razor-sharp concertina wire enclosed the perimeter. Nine Bradley fighting vehicles, five combat vehicles, one tank retrieval vehicle and two Abrams tanks were brought up. The FBI did allow milk to enter for the children, into which they slipped listening devices. By the first of April, "tear gas" had been approved by Clinton; it was not ordinary CN tear gas, but totally different CS: outlawed in war, not for riot control, or in closed structures, emits toxic fumes, flammable.(29)

The final attack began at 6AM, April 19, 1993, as combat vehicles ripped pre-fab walls, injecting gas-spraying booms, spraying "as fast as possible". Fire broke out and the compound exploded in flames as flash-bangs ignited the gas. By 12:41 PM some 80 individuals, including 21 children were burned to a crisp. An Army manual on affects of CS gas, notes, "Generally persons . . . become incapable of executing organized movement".(30) Justice Department investigators could find no evidence for the rationale of Reno's final assault, or the need for gas and tanks. Local police found no cause to be disturbed by Koresh any more than in the case of Randy Weaver. There was no warrant at all to bother the Davidians, let alone to attack and burn them out. A retired FBI agent wrote, "There is not even one fact in the 'probable cause' affidavit . . ." The raid was technically (legal) to serve arrest and search warrants against illegal weaponry, and the Constitution demands "probable cause" as a basis. No attempt was made to serve a warrant, although extensive opportunity existed. The so-called warrants were "sealed by court letter" and were unavailable for over a year.

The Parkland Memorial Hospital received a request from the FBI early April 18, to be prepared to receive a number of burn victims. And the fire department was warned to be ready.(31)

To the remains of the millions of people who went to war "to end the idea that the State should tell people what to believe", it is unbelievable and maddingly cruel to see what "liberals" have done to our country. *Waco Rules of Engagement* is an "impressive documentary" made by two liberal film makers, Dan and Amy Gifford, formerly of CNN. It earned raves at Sundance, a nomination for an Academy Award in documentary, and a press release from Fifth Estate as "illustrating the distrust of the government as no longer confined to right-wing extremists but is firmly rooted in middle America". Film critic Roger Ebert wrote, "You can look in the eyes of the people and tell who is telling the truth".(32) After listening to federal agents boasting of their eagerness to kill the Davidians, you conclude, "if you're looking for unbalanced zealots, you'll find them, not among the Davidians, but among the FBI, the BATF; those are the people to be feared". "Facing a federal lynch mob, the Davidians appealed to reporters to act as witnesses . . . (but) the majority defined as unreasonable any protest over the episode", so commented *The Nation*. Fifty years ago it was believed even by liberals that when "the government becomes a lawbreaker, it breeds contempt for law", or for government even more than law. Now "the government" leads the way.

Hate! Taught hate drove FBI tank drivers to crunch two dozen children's tricycles, bicycles and toys; a dozen motorcycles, cars, a mobile home were crushed by tanks; tires were slashed. A garage was demolished with a tank. Davidian Mike Schroeder was shot Feb. 28 while attempting to rejoin his co-religionists; he was apparently wounded then shot at close range, execution style. When Texas police asked to make casts of footprints and to gather their evidence, FBI commander Jamar refused, and they were not allowed back. A church safe, containing $50,000 in cash plus gold and platinum, survived the fire, was retrieved by the Texas Rangers and signed over to the FBI. It is absent from FBI records, along with its contents. Some of the FBI destruction clearly points to destroying evidence; other to just hate and inhumanness. Freshly filled graves of Davidian victims of Feb. 28, were wantonly desecrated by FBI tanks.(33) Such destruction characterizes not a holocaust of people but an Armageddon of evil, destroying humanness itself.

David Kopel and Paul Blackman wrote an excellent account of the government terrorism in *No More Wacos*. They point out the tyrannical "wartime news control" on the attack. The FBI confiscated film from journalists, had the FCC revoke the broadcast license of KRLD, and refused to release an FBI video. *Rules of Engagement* presents some footage from the FBI tape. The Forward Looking Infrared (FLIR) film footage and critical expert analyses had been given to CBS - *60 Minutes*, but in the end they spiked this important information.

Clinton's Treasury Secretary, under which BATF operated, condemned the Waco "investigation" "as eroding public confidence in government". Some 85 men and women, including 21 children (more than at Oklahoma?), were brutally killed, with no legitimate warrant, according to a former FBI official.

The ravaging of human society has included attacks

not only on education in self government and rule of law; the most damaging and inhuman are those against families, the very building blocks of society for guidance in a culture. These attacks continue on two critical fronts; first in immigration which dilutes and eventually poisons culture; "the danger is balkanization with society increasingly fractured . . . ", R.J. Samuelson.(34) The other front is in the sex revolution and feminism, in destroying families and culture.

Immigration first. Ford Foundation's Mr. Pincus in 1966 funded a Mexican NAACP, the Mexican American Legal Defense and Education Fund, "MALDEF", later creating La Raza. They demand "reconquistia"; Prof. Truxello, of University of New Mexico declared, "We will reclaim our birthright". They demand official recognition of their culture, language, education, and government in Spanish, along with street names, monuments, holidays. Ford head, Maria Obledo, declared, "California is going to be Hispanic. Anyone who doesn't like it should leave". Clinton awarded him his Presidential Medal. Ford, Carnegie, Rockefeller, gave $14 million per year to LaRaza alone. "Look Out Gringo", a *The New Republic* headline 10 years ago.

The Census Bureau, and others, jeer white Americans as "non-Hispanic whites", the media increasingly as non-Semitic whites. A nation of "nons!" The National Education Association was the largest doner to defeat California's Prop 187, to deny illegals welfare; it also seeks tax money to support foreign languages for aliens, before and after they learn English. Ron Unz, in the *Wall Street Journal* claimed for leading university graduates from Harvard to Berkeley: Jews and Asians 50 percent. This leaves about 20 percent for blacks, Moslems, and Mexicans, hence 20 and 10 percent for white females and white males.

In the *Atlantic Monthly*, February 1994, Robert Kaplan described the collapse of organized governments across Africa. Gangs plunder tourists, spread AIDS, TB; the rainforest is cut down, top-soil destroyed, with Martin Van Crevild's grim breakdown of order becoming global.(35) In 1982, the compassionate liberal, Theodore White, assessed the damage done seventeen years earlier by the much praised Immigration Act of 1965, which effectively opened the gates to the Third World. Pouring in beyond quotas, he predicted aliens would be greeted by instant welfare, preferred status and amnesty. Denounced at the time as racist, the truth has soon become apparent. Congressional and media sponsors of the Act had promised: no increase in immigration rates, admission standards held firm, would not redirect immigration away from Europe, would not alter demography. As usual not one liberal promise has been kept.

"An Israeli de Klerk (S. Africa) wouldn't just help birth an independent Palestine; he would do what de Klerk did: tell his people to live as a minority, in someone else's land, in greater Palestine." So wrote Martin Peretz in *The New Republic*,(36) for his country; so too Clinton in America. "Illegal immigration cannot be stopped . . . The destiny of Europe has been settled in North Africa", so claimed the editor of the *Wall Street Journal* last year. So too for America.

It will get worse as long as the mainstream regime: media, government, universities and foundations, provide aliens power and billions of dollars -- $70-90 billions annually from the federal government alone. They have forced a deception, here as usual, that those against destroying our civilization in an alien flood are bigoted "racists", an epithet next to Nazi or anti-Semitic in malignity. And the power of the mainstream to destroy, utterly, has been demonstrated again and again.

Your neighbors may be wonderful people but that gives them no right to take over your house. That our children and young people have been so taught and intimidated, and accept such folly, is a gauge of the mainstream's evil power. It is killing the goose of the golden eggs.

Whether it is better to live like 18th century Zulus or plains Sioux, or as 19th century Europeans is not a realistic question. If Africans, Moslems and others want to live like

Westerners then they must cease insisting that we have nothing to teach them.

Rather than allowing them to drown our civilization, meaning necessarily self governing human societies, we must instead set to helping them up, if they want to live like us. Begin by giving to aliens already here the proper training, then send them back home, with economic help, to build their own more livable societies.

People who understand that civilization is endangered mortally and must be saved for the sake of all humanity must cease complaining; cease arguing with the mainstream, it is a waste of time. Ignore them, and begin to act! Organize with the *intent* to save humanness, and then proceed to rebuild the necessary institutions, as did Christians in the 6th century abbeys.

The other deadly attack upon human society, the sex revolution and feminism, like immigration and all the other attacks upon society, has advanced only through deceptions behind the power of the mainstream, and ignorance. The truth has long been known. Our forebears before conscious reason had no vices, only innate commands; even with conscious reason vices long were rare due to the very visible-to-all implacable need to survive, and necessarily as an "us": a society with standards. After the threat of non-survival was pushed back, man came to recognize that he had to provide his own social restraints. Lack of restraints leads to uncontrolled innate urges: gluttony, sloth, and lust. There are some firm economic and social restraints on gluttony and sloth, but on the most powerful innate urge for sex there is only a social restraint, formerly policed by a shotgun. But now children and people generally are urged to reject any restraints as improper "repressions": bigotry, Victorianism, and so on; not just on "normal" sex but on social perversions, destructive of families and hence of social survival: pederasty, incest, masturbation, bestiality.

We know that what is done is determined by purpose,

and if our purpose is to rise up as human beings in a human society, then families must be protected, and anything destructive of them must be not so much forbidden as taught to be destructive and as justifying contempt.

Socialism arose on Machiavellian promises; the sex revolution and feminism became a part of this wonderful world of idealogy, as powerful tools for "transforming society". Their roots were gathered by Freud, but it was Wilhelm Reich, the Frankfurt School of Jewish Communists, Margaret Mead, and Alfred Kinsey who created the movement, followed by Betty Friedan, nee Goldstein, and many others.

Young humans, particularly males, are virtual animals, and will remain so until taught to be human beings. Society must impose a moral order or there will be disorder and inhumanness. However when people are approached with seductive promises and assured that deprivation of their desires is wrong, followers will always be found. Iagoian voices and untrained or alienated minds there will always be. "Our people today produce criminals, prostitutes, and drunkards, not because it is their nature . . . but because their system of order and tradition has been destroyed", so wrote Alan Paton of South Africa over fifty years ago, to high acclaim. Today the same thing is happening here, with total indifference.

Like nearly all of liberalism, the sex revolution was constructed on lies. The warning given by Euripides in *The Bacchae*, was that the dreams of women who left their homes to dance naked in the hills, "servicing a lover's bed", would end in "horror, suffering and grief". As sex is the most powerful innate demand, "whoever controls sexual behavior will control society", as Euripides and Nietzsche understood. That this lesson has been obscured, as noted by Aldous Huxley in his 1969 preface to *Brave New World*, should now be obvious to all.

There is much complaining about Freud's imaginings passing for science, and of the sexually dysfunctional level of both Freud and his followers, Wilhelm Reich and especially of Alfred Kinsey. But little attention is given to the possibility that

Reich might never have been heard of, had not the prestigious Union Theological Seminary allowed him to be connected to their staff, likewise for Kinsey and John Rock, had they not been financed by Rockefeller money.(37)

Reich was raised in a wealthy East European Jewish family where he was introduced to sex by the maids, perhaps much as was the Gargantua of Rabelais whose nurses would "tickle it under the chin to make it stand." The Weimer Republic, of which Reich saw its ending in 1930 Berlin, was not the mainstream's imagined glorious attempt at German "democracy" which Hitler subverted. It was in many ways quite like America's current "culture", debauched by TV, Hollywood, the media and bureaucracy. Without it and its *Kulturbolschewismus,* along with the real threat of Stalinist bolshevism, Hitler would have remained an unknown.

Reich arrived in New York in 1939, after finding that Stalin wanted no "free love" for his workers. Followers persuaded the New School for Social Research to provide him with thousands of dollars, as Rockefeller support indirectly. His books, *Mass Psychology of Fascism* teaches that repression leads to totalitarianism (opposite to truth), and *The Sexual Revolution* taught that the best way to mobilize youth politically is to promise free sex, "get them sexually active", the motivating force of the 60's revolution. This was also the line taken by the German, Jewish Communists who inspired the "Sixties Student Rebellion": E. Bloch, G. Lukacs, Max Horkheimer, Herbert Marcuse, T.N. Adorno and Walter Benjamin.(38)

Urging them that gratifying their sexual impulses turns them into foot soldiers for "bringing down America", was the strategy of Reich and his followers: Paul Goodman, Alex Lowen, Saul Bellows, and Normal Mailer, and many lesser knowns. Reich was the father of the youth culture and the feminist movement. Kate Millett's *Sexual Politic* (1970) assaulted the traditional family, the whole male patriarchy; Betty Friedan nee Goldstein with an activist Communist past, wrote *The Feminine Mystique.*(1963), and the deceitful "Up from the Kitchen Floor" for *New York Times Magazine* (1973), probably she rarely saw a kitchen floor.

Magnus Hirschfeld, a physician and German Jewish socialist, has been named the "Moses of the homosexual movement"; in 1897 he, publisher Max Spohr, writer Josef von Buelow, and lawyer Ed Oberg founded the *Wissenschaftlich-humantaeres Komittee*, the first homosexual rights organization. In 1919 Hirschfield created the *Institut fuer Sexualwisenschaft* in Berlin, and his name was joined in the popular mind with the moral and cultural corruption of Weimar Germany. His "Institute" became a mecca for voyeurs and perverts of all kinds, as Alfred Kinsey's Indiana Institute for Sex Research was to become.(39)

Kinsey "suggested no way of choosing between women and a sheep" wrote Margaret Mead. A few years ago the editors of *The New Republic* reasoned, "if a person or two or three and a billy goat find a way to be happy that strikes others as revolting, that's no reason for the government to thwart them."(40) However, if the people were truly self governing, it would be they who did the thwarting. Of course, if the billy goat group were to carry out whatever they had in mind in some old barn or their own living room, obviously no one could object. But clearly that was not what the liberal editors had in mind; they wanted "to send a message", "to make a statement"; on TV perhaps a number of programs would have accommodated them.

Kinsey turned "voyeurism into science"; a homosexual sadomasochist, he pushed his wife, colleagues, and visitors into "giving their sexual history" -- for science of course -- and also into engaging in immoral, humiliating and illegal sex, filming when possible. With the noted Columbia Professor, Herbert Wechsler, he launched in the *Harvard Law Review*, May 1952, an attack upon the Constitutional and legal underpinnings of protections against sex predators (today pedophilia and incest are about to fall). The educational arm of the American Bar Association adopted in 1955, a "Model

Penal Code" to alter sex and family laws. Targeted for radical revision were laws on rape, sodomy, bestiality, incest, fornication, indecent exposure, pederasty, and drugs.

Kinsey refused to "publish his basic data . . . not only his hypotheses . . . but facts . . . or to reveal questionnaires". Dr. A.H. Hobbs of the University of Pennsylvania, an early critic, was subjected to "severe persecution" for criticizing Kinsey's data. Kinsey's "scientifically trained observers . . . were perverts . . . who kept detailed records of child molestations and sent to Kinsey", wrote Dr. Judith Reisman, author of *Kinsey, Sex and Fraud* (1990) and *Kinsey*, (1998). She quoted Dr. Lester Caplan, "children had to be held . . . or strapped down, would not respond willingly . . . (A) team of pederasts, experimenters, with records and often photography". Associate Paul Gebhard admitted "It was illegal; we knew it was illegal". One of his "subjects", Mr. Green, admitted molesting 800 boys and girls over many years. When Dr. Reisman exposed Kinsey at the 1981 Fifth World Conference on Sexology in Jerusalem, she expected her colleagues to be enraged; instead they turned on her with vicious denunciation.(42)

"Looking back it seems astounding that the American public accepted any of Kinsey's findings, all of which conflicted with public health reports . . . (and) what Americans heard, saw, or knew about their homes, schools, children, friends . . . " "Not only has Kinsey and his associates (many, like Reich, Hirschfeld, and sex writers male and female, from Goodman, Mailer, Bellows, and John Heidenry of *Wild Ecstacy* to Lisa Polac, Eliz Wurtzel, Sally Tisdale, also Christopher Isherwood, and mass murderers John Wayne Gacy and Jeffrey Dahmer, and most of the rest are alleged or admitted homosexuals) escaped prosecution . . . and condemnation . . . for unspeakable acts"(43); there is even more. "Almost all AIDS and sex education, from elementary to post-graduate, is based on Kinsey's 'variant' sex model", so claimed Dr. Reisman.

The New York *Times* reported the first showing of Kinsey's "erotic art". Entirely donated, it ranged from the "academic", to what *Times* sensitively labeled "the unschooled", crude, mass porn. Gallery director Betsy Sterrat commented. "People look so intently . . . get up close . . . takes every day cleaning." *Times* judged it "decorous", "appealing to both sexes . . . while eschewing zoophilia".(41)

In Massachusetts schools under Governor Wm. Weld's "Safe School Program", anyone who "opposes" the teaching of homosexuality lifestyles as a normal way of life, even on religious and moral grounds will be prosecuted. So goes First Amendment religious and speech guarantees without a murmur. Even at Notre Dame's Saint Mary's College a Holy Cross nun, Sister Linda Cors, CSC, led a dozen or so Catholic coeds in Eve Ensler's *Vagina Monologues*, in which "the girls work up a sweat chanting, or croaking like Aristophanes' *Frogs*, C ---, C ---, C ---, C ---, C --- . . . to the Saint Mary's audience of young Catholic ladies. The accompanying play included, "I worried about my vagina", until she realized "My vagina is me." Others, "Home is a very scary place" (Her father is paying $20,000 a year for this). "Shelters are the place women find comfort with other women." A 13 year old girl being sexually molested by an older woman is graphically portrayed most compassionately. So reported Catholic writer E. Michael Jones who was there.(44)

This, and much more like it, is but a part of the regime's plan (it wouldn't exist unless supported) to "break down the defense against exploitation which modesty provides . . . Colonization takes place by inculcating bad habits, then organizing those habits politically into a movement like feminism". "St. Mary's . . . calls itself Catholic but is run by feminists, who do the bidding of foundations and government agencies that support their sexual compulsions for political reasons."(45) Music and drama, much like reason, are powerful teachers, either to corrupt or to edify as Plato warned. Thus the Cincinnati Museum Director Dennis Barrie was publicly "honored" for being one of the first to show Maplethorpe's child molestations and hard core homoeroticism.

People ultimately will always demand an escape from corruption and chaos, and there will always be ruthless brutes ready to lead them into a servitude. Society seeks to maintain order mildly by awarding respect or contempt; when society is destroyed tyrannical leaders do it with terror and servitude. All the great "liberation" movements of the past centuries have provided the destructive forces for totalitarianism. Our regime has found no strategies more powerful in destroying human society than the alien flood and sexual liberation. Most women can see that sex lib has brought pain, suffering, loneliness and depression, while for centuries people found uplift, joy, hope and contentment in the institutions of humanness: religion, literature, families.

NOTE ON RACISM

"Racism", unlisted as a word in OED, is defined in Webster's Collegiate as a "belief that race is the primary determinant of human traits and capacities". This is dissembling; innateness if primary could be no more a "belief" than is hunger. People are taught when and how to eat, and can be taught when race is non-threatening.

There is much evidence that the entire world is entering an age of pronounced ethnicity, not just in Africa, but in Asia, the Balkans, Great Britain, and now in America. As religion and nations falter only blood-bonds remain, before global terror enslaves all. Everything human originated and will survive only in a society, organized to achieve that as a primary purpose. "Us" - "them" is innate in all societies: insects, birds, and mammals. Well into historic times a distrust and fear of "them" was commonly justified. Civilization, as man's organized attempt to mitigate the human prospect, has urged reason as a replacement for force in settling disputes. Principal efforts have been carried out through religion and culture. Liberal renegades today seek to annihilate the "us-them" dichotomy with multiculturalism, which can be achieved only with the destruction of society itself and of humanness, their admitted and obvious goal. It is a measure of the malignity of modern liberals that they have used a "taught hatred", or racism, to intimidate those who reject their bureaucratic tyranny.

Slavery arose from the us-them separation; natural law collateral with society applied only *within* society, and killing or enslaving others was permitted or even commanded. Abject slavery is most characteristic of Africa; read the account of a black slave of Moslems in the 1930s by Antoine de Saint Exupéry, in *Wind, Sand and Stars*.(1) In Asia it has been more commonly family oppression and in Europe servitude for defeated people. Enslavement of black Africans by Arabs extends back into pre-history; note that slaves of Arabs left no posterity as they did in America. And Dr. Livingstone was not lost; he had been working for years to close down Arab-Black slave markets. Slavery was terminated after ages of existence principally by Christian fundamentalist and evangelical churches, as the Methodist Church at that time. Today the renegade media jeers at the Biblical acceptance of slavery, while never noting the lack of effort by Enlighteners or Marxists to uproot it.

Blacks played an important part in collecting and in transporting slaves, as documented by Dr. Amanda Lee Brooks.(2) She also showed that many blacks, when freed by their owners, used their education and connections to enter the lucrative slave trade. As did Cinqué of *Amistad* fame; his liberty was granted by a Court predominantly Southern.(3) The trade was lucrative because decent people would not enter, as Lincoln noted.(4)

Read also of the harassment and intimidation that Dr. Brooks was subjected to by "liberal intellectuals" while doing her thesis research on the unpermissible: black schools named for black slave traders, the forcing of ex-slaves into a radicalisms, West African women networking the slave trade, and much more. The first Negro republics, such as Haiti, born of a murderous slave rebellion and U.S. established Liberia, quickly opened a thriving slave trade. Today a large majority of black children are victimized by grossly substandard education, through the connivance of local black politicians seeking money, the NEA reaching for political power, and the Democratic Party harvesting votes.

The people of Africa in the 18th and 19th centuries, who often sold some of their own children into slavery (or cannibalism) for an umbrella or piece of red cloth, were of a culture somewhere between stone-age American Indians and even more primitive Australian aborigines. Lincoln insisted they were not equal to whites culturally.(5)

A *Washington Post* correspondent, Keith Richburg, made an extended study of Africa some five years ago. He reported bodies "stacked like firewood". Rwanda as in prehistoric times, "a sick version of Fred Flintstone . . . smashing skulls and chopping off limbs . . . legs in one pile, arms in another . . . human beings don't do things like that . . . cavemen". Bodies floating in the river . . . hundreds of thousands. "I was seeing all this horror . . . I am an American . . . descendent of slaves . . . these nameless, faceless bodies washing over a waterfall, piled in the back of trucks . . . look like me . . . Simply as I know, 'There but for the grace of God (and America) go I'".(6)

Richburg denied European colonization as an excuse; look at Asian colonies ruled for 300 years. Ghana had been the Gold Coast due to mineral wealth, and was Africa's brightest hope at independence with a higher GNP than South Korea, which was devastated by war in the Fifties and burdened since with defense. Today Korea is an economic powerhouse, while Ghana has a GNP lower than at independence.

Richburg, along with the *Wall Street Journal* and others have searched for *"why"*. The answer is quite simple, it was written by Alan Paton in 1948. "It is not permissible to go on destroying family life when we know we are destroying it . . . The old tribal system" for all its faults "was a moral system. Our people today produces criminals, prostitutes and drunkards, not because it is their nature . . . but because their system of order and tradition (their society) has been destroyed . . . We have an inescapable duty" to rebuild a system of order.(7)

      The horror is not only that it has never been rebuilt in Africa; such an order (society) is being destroyed in most of the West, with consequences that could be far worse than in Africa. Jim Sleeper condemned "the overthrow of civic culture (in New York) . . . for the sake of liberation . . . (it) wins not justice but more death". Black leaders should determine whether the hatred expressed by so many blacks in America is not a somewhat civilized reflection of that exemplified so obviously in Africa.

      America fought its most terrible war to free black people who had been enslaved by their own people; men from the North however entered Lincoln's war against the South to save the Union. But by the mid-1870s it was becoming clear that the saved-Union was much different from the remembered. After the feculent 14th Amendment, no longer would "All that pertains to life, liberty and property" be determined by the people in their own communities. The State became a regime. By 1936, Lippmann realized that a new collectivist establishment had subverted our human society.

      A case may be made that most wars are instigated by intellectuals, as were the French and American Revolutions, and certainly the Civil War. Far more intense dislike of the negro existed in the North than in the South, and the Abolitionists had little real sympathy for black people and only hatred for Southerners. They demanded secession, "They take one away, we t' other", and made no effort to support peaceful abolition. But the horror of the Civil War and the subsequent illegal imposition of the feculent 14th Amendment were only the beginning. Intellectuals either supported or did not oppose the madman Thad Stevens who sought to impose a tyrannical parliamentary system with no Bill of Rights, as was openly charged at the time.(8)

      The gradual subversion of our Constitutional government continued; by 1900, C.A. Beard was to write, "in power the States had become but shadows of their former selves." During and following WW I's disruptions, the Court assumed control of free speech and press -- a violation of the Bill. By

1954 the Court brazenly stripped away the final vestiges of rule of law -- in critical Constitutional issues; instead of declaring the Constitution color blind, as asked and as responsibility required, the Court took the opportunity to grab a precedent for total supremacy over law, government, and people. Soon it would arrogantly stand forth and declare the right of Communists to teach subversion, to work in defense plants, to be immune from FBI observation, and to deny religion which all our Founders had declared essential for self government a presence in the public square.

Thus the philosophy and practice of humanness was replaced by the senseless hand of the bureaucratic State. Welfare engineering is closely related to the "war on reason". Jacob Riis, an immigrant New York police reporter was an early "social environmentalist"; he denied the moral responsibility of the poor. But environment provided for him only an explanation, not an excuse. Social amelioration was not to be superficial, as with a dole; it was to accomplish a transformation, a lifting of people up to humanness. Pauperism's dole was incompatible with self respect (a given when I grew up).(9)

Then a deep social shift began, led by Lippmann's 1936 new establishment; the perception was forced that moral reform was but a tool for "capitalist" oppression, not the doorway to progress and humanness. In 1978, David Rothman explained that movements which had been labeled reform on humanitarian aspects, were now criticized and damned for seeking to control behavior. "We are witnessing the breakdown of normality", he went on, and denied that we can or ought to attempt to restore it.(9) Denial of humanness has promoted inhumanness, divorce, crime, with racism exalted to victimhood. Thirty years ago the NY *Times* wrote of "parading perverts"; today eminent psychiatrists are attacked for seeking to relieve homosexual distress with proven reparative therapy. And police who have put their lives in jeopardy to arrest dangerous felons have been subjected to long prison sentences. These identify not irrationality but renegadism.

"Racism" has become a two-edged sword for liberal renegades: a club for beating down opposition, and a torch to spread burning hatred, as Sowell has been quoted. Bernard Goetz was a slender, 37 year old electrical engineer who often used the notorious violence-prone New York subway. As commonly carrying expensive instruments and cash he applied for and was denied a carry-gun permit, though he had previously been assaulted and sustained serious injury; the police tried to accuse him of picking the fight, with three black thugs. Dec. 22, 1984 four young muggers, actually legal adults with arrest records and one awaiting trial, began their "playing with" Goetz, asking him for $5 with sharpened screw-drivers visible. Goetz shot the four punks, not critically; as they lay bleeding he calmly helped a hysterical lady to a seat, spoke briefly to the conductor and disappeared, until giving himself up some five days later.

The incident would very likely never have been widely noted except for the fact that "from day-one . . . hundreds of people called police to support Goetz". The "subway vigilante" was the talk of talk radio. Almost totally the subway riders, especially the black women, sided with Goetz; 8 percent of New Yorkers had been mugged in the past year, 31 percent burglarized. People weren't afraid of vigilantes; they feared and hated muggers. Police-posted composite photos grew drawn-in halos.(10)

Liberals bristled in reaction at "vigilantism" with increasing palpitations as letters-to-the-editor and talk-shows burgeoned with felicitous comments. Mayor Koch hired 1300 extra police to track down the criminal and warned that "that sort of thing had led to the Holocaust." Gov. Cuomo had his condemnation. Perhaps Goetz overreacted, but when the most basic function of government is abandoned, what is one to do? Goetz had made a direct hit on the issue of the legitimacy of the renegade regime. Even CORE's Roy Innes offered to raise defense money.

It is not vigilantism when criminals pursue you. The Probation Department criticized Goetz's "obsessions with being victimized" -- like Jimmy Carter's "inordinate fear". Goetz's Prosecutor, "you should go somewhere's else where your fragile sensibilities will not be assaulted". The government tells a citizen to make way for criminals. The great majority of subway riders agreed with the black mother who was afraid of the "punks who were bothering the white man . . . they got what they deserved."

Minorities, the poor and disadvantaged, even Goetz's muggers, have serious problems, made worse by welfare, corrupt education and the renegade media. Boys who kill, youths who mug and shoot, the criminals who attack police -- in LA, Miami, Cincinnati, New York, everywhere -- have not been brought up, educated for society, and not informed as to what will not be allowed, nor of the miraculous opportunities available in human society.

In the Nineties Jeffrey Snyder's essay "A Nation of Cowards"(11) argued, "Crime is rampant because *we* (e.a.) condone it. *We* encourage it when we do not fight back. *We* are cowards and shirkers." As noted previously the mainstream refuses to admit the Manichaean split of the "We" of the mainstream from Goetz, the black women, and the populace which they loathe.

A couple years ago a Michigan black boy who lived with male relatives in a dope (and worse) den, took one of their guns to school and blew the head off of a beautiful six year old white girl who had spurned his advances. A couple years before that a black youth went out to "shoot someone", which he did, a white boy he didn't know. In 1991 a 15 year old black youth heaved a cement block on to the Ford Freeway, killing a 29 year old mother. In June, 1965, I was heading west on Interstate 80 through South Chicago near a J.F. Kennedy overpass in a station wagon with my wife and 4 children. As I approached some underpass, I noted a group of a half dozen black women and as many children move out onto the overpass. A boy came to the rail, waited, then heaved down a round stone half the size of his head. It hit the cement, bounced up and hit the heavy bumper (in those days) with a bang. A fraction of a second later, we might all have been dead.

A number of years after that I was uncomfortably finessed into doing a good turn for a black women, well-dressed and apparently with a good job. I ended up on her screened porch with her black "friend", and was about to leave, when a two foot high black child rushed into the room, saw me, his eyes saucered -- really -- and zip he was gone. Turning to go he was back, walked to the center of the room and with chest out, "We'ze blak foks, Wee don lik white foks!" The man guffawed, the woman's eyes hardened and I left.

Little short of barbarism can be found to match the failure of late 20th century U.S. to provide simple justice and social order. The Mimses were a poor, elderly, disabled, white couple of Manning, S.C., he with asthma and a bad back and she with diabetes, for whom prison terms of 10 years were sought. Their son had regularly played with a black boy, both pre-teens. One day Mims accused the black boy, Dwight Miller, of taking something from his truck, whereupon Dwight went home.

Six hours later, the Millers told the police that Mims had tied Dwight to a tree with a belt around his neck, hit him with a crowbar, fired a shotgun past his head, and had threatened to kill his entire family. Dwight was taken to an emergency room where doctors reported no visible signs or marks, nothing at all.

At a trial the Mimses, their boy and another boy, steadfastly denied any assault. There was no physical evidence; no marks, no crowbar, no shotgun blasted tree nor shot heard, while there was strong evidence that Mims was incapable of even catching the 10 year old black boy. But the NAACP brought in a special prosecutor, packed the courtroom with "black leaders", supporters, and media. Few courts when thus intimidated and faced with New York lawyers are willing to stick their necks out. It was a "reparations lynching", with two poor, disabled, illiterates on the block, given mercy sentences of two years in prison. How like the many child-abuse cases.(12)

John Rocker said of New York's #7 train's patrons nothing racist or hateful, just what he looked askance at, as do most Americans, and he too discovered Tom Wolfe's "most intense vilification", and nearly exclusion from his profession with hardly a voice raised to support him. When Bryant Gumbel cursed a supporter of the Court's decision on Boy Scouts, "what a f - - - - - - idiot", not a media murmur was raised.

New Jersey's governor Whitman fired 35-year veteran Police Superintendent for suggesting that minorities are more likely to be involved in drug trafficking. And a Supreme Court dismissed criminal charges against 19 blacks, claiming a "policy of targeting blacks", regardless of the fact they essentially all had been convicted by black jurors. But Jesse Jackson thanked his lucky stars that the footsteps behind him were of white people. Now's that profiling.

Jesse Jackson, Spike Lee, Toni Morrison, and many others have become rich and famous for peddling "blackface holocaust" with slavery and victimhood "into the big-time martyr context," so Stanley Crouch charged. And Jim Sleeper wrote of New York's "civic culture . . . of admiration for excellence . . . the main engine of black progress", much like Booker T. Washington whom the socialist's NAACP denigrated. It was the New York media that began paying big money and giving celebrity for "claim-making rooted in race . . . destroyed the shared civic culture that made tolerance possible".

The real problem, as has been reiterated, is not racism; which is natural; the real problem is the destruction of human society which will lead to far greater horrors than racism. Lyrics for Ice-T's "Home Invasion", according to Time-Warner's jacket description, has a white teenager listening raptly while black thugs beat his father and rape his mother. One would think young people would be revolted by such a corrupt picture of them.

Consider Spike Lee as featured in *Newsweek*. He's cool, "not afraid to deal with anything . . . drugs, passion". Not Spike, except human decency and truth. *Newsweek* quotes Spike, "What it comes down to is white males have problems with black men's sexuality . . . we've got a hold on their women". "White bitches . . . throwing themselves at black men . . . (even old Vernon had to settle for a whore, and most for rape) self hating black men (poor things) can't deal with black women". Not even original; remember Julius Lester's "Look out whitey! Black Power's Gon' Git Yo Mami!"

If white men have problems with black men's sexuality, and white women are such lays, how come black men raping white girls is dozens of times greater than white men, of which there are many more, raping black girls?

Spike Lee is not just a dissembler and a racist provocateur, he is a threat to both white and black society, pimping for Hollywood. "Lee deals with passion . . . hottest topic of the *'Jungle'*." Angie Sciorra is tired of "her sensitive boy friend . . . she's been told black men know how to f--k . . . a delicately tender performance". A full page *Newsweek* spread, all in color, bra askew, eyes glazed, spread out on the drawing table, with old Flipper pounding away.(13)

Then comes Angie's "shocked, *racist* (e.a.) father, brother, and long time boyfriend . . . beaten and banished by her father; then she and Flipper are cast out by his (non-racist) father . . . (as) whore mongers." Not "meant to represent every interracial couple (Newsweek hastens to emphasize) . . . just a sexual mythology". Like Oliver Stone's *JFK, Nixon*, etc., historical mythology, intended to mock human society. These renegades "loathe the society they rule", wrote David Gelernter in *Commentary*. Shelby Steele called it a liberal lie that Malcolm X's father was killed and his house burned by the KKK. He had received an eviction notice and burned his own house.(14)

There is much truth in Stephen and Abigail Thernstrom's, and others', insistence on "One America", but it is far from the whole truth, in fact doesn't touch the controlling factors. Very few whites desire or dare a confrontation with blacks; somewhat reciprocally Tom Sowell claimed that 58 percent of L.A. blacks looked on the Rodney King looters as disgraceful.

The truth is that "hate" is but a tactic, developed by Marx and socialists generally, for destroying society for the enthronement of the State, and used by ADL, SPLC, ACLU, BATF, Jackson, and Sharpton to raise money. This is the "Change" that has been pushed, from Marx to Clinton. An article by Harvard's psychiatry professor, A.F. Poussant, in Jewish *Forward*, charged that "Some individuals angrily resist change." Clearly "liberal change" constitutes their agenda for destruction of families, rule of law, humanness, and self government, and when people see their civilization being attacked they have a duty to resist the "change". This is never considered; the issue is presented as the mainstream renegade "we" against the Nazis and nativists. A prominent New York rabbi declared, "Look, you people are making this too complicated. They're Yahoos and rednecks, racists and Klu Kluxers, and we're not. That's all there is to it".(15)

Lifetime communist activist Gordon Allport set the tone for Sara Bullard's *Teaching Tolerance*, which has not a single white victim or non-white perpetrator. There is an associated racist video, "The Shadow of Hate". Similarly ADL and Barnes and Noble are pushing a book, *Hate Hurts*, which also demonizes whites. Morris Dees's $100 million dollar SPLC hate center has pushed *Teaching Tolerance* into 50,000 schools. Schools routinely refuse a balancing program to accompany these on "white hate".

The NEA representative to a national conference on homosexuality in school curricula in Atlanta in 1999, Deanna Duby, explained "The religious right fears that the schools of today will be the government of tomorrow. And do you know what, they're right".(16)

Halls of learning have become "reeducation camps" where "diversity educators" teach "sensitivity" even as they teach white students to feel guilty, and to hate themselves and their civilization. Prominent among these is Jane Elliot; she teaches that "white people invented racism", and are a parasitic race who stole everything from other races, even the English language. Her film "Blue Eyed" teaches white students, and even their parents at orientations, self contempt and blood guilt. She receives $6,000/daily plus expenses from schools, companies, and government agencies to teach hate. Imagine the government paying six cents for teaching Christianity or even humanness. Disney plans a movie of her life.(17)

Last year the TV Discovery Channel had a three hour "hate" program, wherein all the purveyors of racial hate and all perpetrators were white, and all victims non-white. In 1993 a gang of blacks, after watching the movie "Mississippi Burning", attacked a white boy; he was in a coma for four days and permanently disabled. In 1999, a group of blacks watched "A Time to Kill," and went out and stomped to death a 50 year old retarded white person. "Rosewood" and "Hurricane" are films that would never have seen day, with colors reversed. A movie a couple years back, was based on a real incident, except the "good guy" was changed from white to black and the "bad" from black to white. The California 1999 Hate Crime Report contains pictures of four events, all with white perpetrators and non-white victims; the same pictures are repeated four times. The "racist dragging to death" of James Byrd in Texas was a crime of revenge for years of humiliation and rape in Texas prisons; had the prison rapists been Mexican so too would have been the revenge victim. In that sense it is wrong to perceive it as racist; the real criminal was the government that knowingly allowed such a scandal.

And what is the truth? The U.S. Department of Justice report gives 1,276,030 violent, interracial crimes for 1999. In 90 percent of the interracial crimes, the victim was white, and in 98 percent of interracial rapes, the victims were white. The major FBI requirement for a legal "hate" crime is that it be interracial. In 1998 the FBI listed nine "hate crimes", of which five victims were white. The Los Angeles County Hate Crime Report listed nine racially motivated murders or attempted murder, none committed by whites. Between 1995 and 1999 the FBI reviewed 475 cases for possible capital punishment; there were 95 white perpetrators of which 36 were marked for capital punishment (38%). Of the 380 non-white perpetrators, 85 cases (22%) were recommended for death row. Keep in mind the far greater total number of whites. California's State Criminal Information for 1997 reported 1761 arrests for murder, with 1298 non-white criminals, 361 white; yet 3 of 5 whites were given capital punishment.

On Seattle's Mardi Gras, Feb, 27, 2001, over 75 non-whites selected whites to be beaten, sexually assaulted, and in at least one case murdered, all documented on TV and citizen videos, while police were ordered not to enter the heavy crime area. The man murdered, Chris Kime, was defending a white women from non-white thugs hurling racial epithets. The Mayor, City Council, and Police Chief (not street officers), the Seattle *Times*, and the *Post-Intelligencer,* all denied the attacks were "racial" and sought to censure it from the Internet. "Professors" were paid to declare "no racial crisis". See Ref. 17A. However by August 2001 the Seattle FBI confirmed that they would open an investigation of the riot, focusing on the question of motivation and conspiracy.

It will also focus on whether the City of Seattle, the County District Attorney, and others, conspired "under the color of law" to deny citizens the protection of state hate crime laws. Another FBI criterion for a "hate crime" is whether the city leaders are fearful of being labeled a hate crime city (more than fearful of injustice), and another concerns whether the force used is far in excess of that for robbery.

In Wichita, Dec. 7, 2000, two young black Carr brothers abducted white Andrew Schreiber from a Kum and Go Market, took him to an ATM and robbed him, and allegedly "assaulted him with a gun", perhaps for hours, the details of which were ordered locked by a court, censoring the humiliation and debasing atrocities. The Carr brothers then on Dec 11, accosted and shot in the face, Wichita Orchestra cellist Ann Walenta outside her home. On the 15th they invaded an upscale townhouse, kidnapped five young whites, stole their pickup and drove them to an ATM where they were robbed, then driven to an isolated field, stripped and raped both women, and forced them into censored sex acts, including the three man. Satiated they forced all five to kneel and shot each in the head execution style. Miraculously one of the women regained consciousness, walked naked a mile in December snow for help.

Here as in Seattle, community leaders conspired to keep the truth hidden. The County Attorney obtained a court order sealing the prosecution's case, the Wichita *Eagle* so noted on Dec. 30 and by Jan. 7 came out with a "no racist" white-wash. A priest and a professor were found to preach forgiveness and to declare no racial issue.

It is quite easy to determine from police questioning whether the regime wants the truth or not. Ask the Carrs leading questions that would bring out racial animus; tell one something and the other something else, then reverse the story. State and local officials formed a Hate Crime Task Force following an incident in 1998, but it has so far been silent. Most people know of James Byrd, but who ever heard of the Carr Brothers? The horror is that no one cares -- no one knows, unless the victim is black or Jew and the attacker a white male. There was the brutal stabbing of a Utah tourist; a 30 years old son of a Washington, D.C. black mother working two jobs to support him, killed her by forcing an iron rod up her rectum, for more money; a woman dragged to her death under a car; Mrs. Weaver holding her baby in her arms and shot in the face. On and on; no one really cares.

The amelioration of hate is not attained in more hate but in *truth*, and in comprehension. Scholars from Nietzsche, Tocqueville, Nobelist Schweitzer, to C.S. Lewis and Samuel Livingston have warned of the suicide of our civilization. Yet liberals, particularly in the universities and media, openly insist upon the necessity for change, meaning destruction of human civilization. The "vast right-wing conspiracy", formerly the "moral majority", consisted of the productive common people who resisted attacks upon their human society. The media -- *Times, Post,* and networks -- the universities and much of the church hierarchy insist upon the bigotry, racism, and necessary annihilation of the right-wing common people whom, they force the perception of being allied with KKK and Nazis. The beginning of these distortions, lies, and taught hatred, comes with the likes of Bullard's dissembling and bigoted *Teaching Tolerance.*

People don't recognize anti-social propaganda when they see it. "Amos 'N Andy" were ousted as a bigoted portrayal of black people, although it actually showed many more good traits and none truly bad; "the purpose of playing . . . is to hold a mirror up to nature." Today we have the hateful distortions of Oliver Stone, Norman Lear, and others. Recently there was the movie "Brotherhood of Murder", described in the *Wall Street Journal* as "frothing malignance, lurid Aryan conceits . .. mind encrusted with hate".

These attacks are all concealed assaults on America' human society. The only KKK member I ever met was Harry Truman, or knew of as a person was the very liberal Supreme Court Justice Hugo Black. We constantly receive reports of KKK activities but people would be astonished at how many of the incidents were hoaxes, like the vast Southern black church burnings, or Olympic victim Jewell, or were acts performed by *provocateurs*, as charged in FDR's "Sedition Trial". J.F. Kennedy's assassination was blamed on "Right-Wing Extremists", even by the Warren Commission. The question is as to whether Oswald, whose recent connections with the KGB, and Communist parties in Cuba and Mexico were well know, acted under Communist orders, and if so why would the Left have sought to eliminate Kennedy? Was it not to cover the inevitable chaos in Vietnam which was certain to follow the American Left's assassinations and destruction of their government leaders?

The Arizona Amtrack derailment in 1995, the Starr and McCranie case of Georgia, Ruby Ridge and Waco, the Vipers Team of Phoenix, Oklahoma, and more were all hoaxes or had *provocateurs* involved. All lead to loud cries of right-wing terrorists all the way to the White House, carried by the ADL, Morris Dees of SPLC and Joe Roy of Klan Watch. But there are also Ken Stern of Am. Jewish Comm., and John Natter of the Conflict Analysis Group. Millionaire Dees started out as a segregationist White Council lawyer; however he soon found the prospects for money much brighter on the other side.

Americans see their civilization being destroyed; they have a right and a duty to resist and to hate, but should instead rebuild. If negro riots were payback, so was Oklahoma. The purpose here is to show and explain a far better and more certain way to regain our self governing human society. Part of the motivation must come from comprehension of what has been going on.

Last year, the Quigleys of Evergreen, Colorado were awarded $10.5 million in damages from the ADL. Briefly, what Jefferson County District Attorney Thomas called "a neighborhood dispute" was blown out of all proportion by the ADL and its media power. The Quigleys were arrested and charged with a felony, suffered harassment for anti-Semitism; their reputations were ruined and they received death threats. Their Jewish neighbors, the Aronsons, had been coaxed into a hoax by the ADL, for which they too are now suing ADL.(18)

This and other incidents followed Abe Foxman's ADL publication on the *Religious Right* which linked principled conservatives with KKK, Nazis, and bigotry. Gary Pollard an ADL leader joined with 75 prominent Jews in signing a full page *New York Times* advertisement for Aug. 2, 1994 criticizing the ADL for "defamation of its own" (Pollard?), against the "religious right". ADL cast Pollard from its ranks for taking a stand against "defamation".

In the Fifties America was confident, compassionate, proud, and rising. In the years since, Aryans have been demeaned to non-Hispanic whites, whimpish, sub-adults, ashamed of their history, fearful of having "chests", little more than emasculates. Rather than confident as inheritors of Aryan civilization, they are intimidated into a demeaned status as "non-Semitic whites" by the media, thus declaring that what once were normally considered as Aryans, you and me, have become nameless non-persons. I refuse to be a hyphenated non-Hispanic white, Indo-European, or Anglo, even if the word Aryan, founders of Western civilization, has been made more reprehensible than nigger or kike; it was socialists who advertised and misused the name "Aryan" to gain adherents, and later blackening it to damn Western civilization.

Socialists developed the concept of Aryan superiority. All European languages and therefore peoples had been found to have developed from a culture from which even Sanskrit had evolved. Western civilization was therefore derived from what came to be known as Aryan culture, and socialists created the concept of Aryan superiority as a tactic for drawing followers while denigrating inferior races: the origin of modern taught racism.(19) Marx's competitor in leading German socialism was Ferdinand Lassalle whose kinky type of hair led Marx to refer in a letter to Engels to "the Jewish Nigger Lassalle . . . the obtrusiveness of the fellow is also nigger-like".(20)

Lenin praised Marx's paper "On the Jewish Question",(21) as signaling Marx's transition from idealistic socialism to Communism and "class struggle". "What is the secular cult of the Jews? Huckstering." His criticism was directed not at Sabbath Jews but at Jewish capitalists. He also saw "The practical domination of Judaism over the Christian world . . . "(22) And Marx, "Now for the first time Judaism could gain universal supremacy . . . "(23)

Then as the 19th century ended there were again basic alterations in socialism. First, many educated Jews had been moving into the Marxian branch which was to become Communism; the Christian Socialists excluded Jews. Hence Communists decreased or keep hidden their anti-Semitism. Second, E.A. Ross in his *Sociology* of 1905 wrote of "the Negro . . . who in strength of appetites and power to control them differs considerably from the white man", but in his 1929 *Sociology*, "Given our training, their minds would work as ours". Socialists came to recognize that black people could be used to spread hatred in society, and had created in 1909 the NAACP; by 1911, they had W.E.B. DuBois to front-offices for them. It was not until 1975 that there would be an NAACP black president. Their intent was to replace the self-help work of Booker T. Washington with radical social unrest. Third, before 1900 the socialists retained a belief in the solid virtues of the Middle Ages with their "chartered freedom . . . and idyllic relations between men" which had produced idealist socialism as noted by Marx.(24) Socialism beginning as "a reactionary protest against a new and poorly understood economic movement (industrial capitalism), (was) an appeal to turn the clock backwards" to "good medieval doctrine" and order(25). This was now stoutly rejected for a new line that denied any connection to the Middle Ages; rather "capitalism was . . . the true parent of socialism".(26)

These changes which were taking place as the 19th was changing into the 20th century were undoubtedly influenced by the Dreyfus Affair. In France socialist Charles Fourier's violent anti-Semitism was followed by Alphonse Toussenel, whose *Les Juifs* claimed that the "universal domination, dreamed of by conquerors, the Jews have in their hand".(27) Jewish socialist Edouard Drumond's periodical, *Libre Paroles*, laid the basis for the railroading of Captain Dreyfus. And in Jan. 1898 the French socialist press published a manifesto for "non-participation in the Dreyfus affair . . . the reaction exploits the conviction of one Jew to disqualify all Jews . . . Jews use the rehabilitation of a single Jew to wash out all the 'stains of Israel'".(28)

Signers of the manifesto included Jean Jaures, the leading French socialist orator, who was to be noted (mistakenly?) for his "mighty efforts . . . on the side of Dreyfus".(29) Jaures was to write the very famous line: "These Jews closely knit together . . . separated from other men as enemies . . . isolated by blood, religion, lucrative profession, and by a common hate for the rest of humanity, who control all business, all wealth, who bend free men under the yoke of money. What is Jewry if not *a dangerous State within a State?*" (e.a.)(30)

Marx made one more notable contribution to taught hatred: the tactic of "one enemy", with one class blamed for all faults and social failures, "identical with the notorious crimes of society".(31) Hitler took this up, giving Marx full credit and noted that "one enemy" "greatly increased the bitterness".(32) It is bizarre that the one enemy of both should have been a "Judaistic manifestation".

There is so much more concerning the great evil done by socialists in the past century which cannot be covered here, but genocide cannot be ignored. "Racial extermination" and "genocide on socialist grounds" has been documented in articles by both Marx and Engels.(33) "The chief mission of other races . . . is to perish in the revolutionary holocaust . . . what progress means".(34) Hermann Rauschning was told by Hitler that National Socialism was based on Marx.(35) H.G. Wells and G.B. Shaw both long time socialists declared that the ideal of equality required, obviously, mass-killing of the unfit. Shaw's preface to *On the Rocks* (1933), headed "Extermination", urged "a scientific basis".

The great horror of the past century has been the application of these ideas to practice by Stalin, Hitler, Mao, aided in most cases by American socialists and by Franklin Roosevelt -- even Hitler was loaned large sums of money. Yet our media and entertainment presents only the evil of the

American people: Oliver Stone's "Born on the Fourth", "Scarface", "Salvador", "Platoon" and more. In *JFK* America is presented as a fascist state. Norman Lear and Ed Asner present hate and degradation of America as comedy. Why not a Jew or black once in a while for an Archie Bunker. And Wm. Greider bleats, "Behind the formal shell is a systematic breakdown of the shared civil value. Power has gone to the few."(36)

During the radical Weimar period of pre-Hitler Germany, a Jewish millionaire founded the Frankfurt School to "transform research directly into socialist propaganda". By late Thirties, T.W. Adorno, Eric Fromm, Herb Marcuse, and Max Horkheimer had moved to U. Calif. Berkeley and in 1950 produced *The Authoritarian Personality*,(37) before returning to postwar Germany. Their works and followers in America guided Lenin's idiots in their Sixties' ravishing of humanness, introduced recreational sex, sowed the seeds of political correctness, and led Jewish organizations to identify traditional human values with incipient "Fascism"" -- post modernism. They targeted anything that supported families, social coherence, and humanness, while promoting "rebellion against parents, casual sex, scorn for upward mobility, family pride, patriotism, and religion." All these pathologies were only for others, not for Jews.

The socially destructive ideas of Franz Boas, provided intellectual support for greatly increased immigration, racial integration, inter-racial marriage, and a perceived white oppression of minorities. Prof. Charles Silberman wrote of "Jews committed to cultural tolerance", "approval of homosexuality", and "diversity". Brandeis University's President, Earl Raab, expressed satisfaction with a coming white minority status, "We've tipped beyond the point where Western civilization can continue to prevail". All these actions for destroying human society and Western civilization are presented in a three volume *Culture of Critique* by Kevin MacDonald.(38)

"After the Bolshevik Revolution the Jewish presence became intolerable to European religious and political elites who regarded Bolshevism as a Jewish assault on Christendom," so wrote R.L. Rubenstein (39), author of *After Auschwitz*. Left hanging is the question "Was the belief in a Jewish assault" justified, and did "The Holocaust" follow from it? Mr. Rubenstein and nearly all Holocaust theologians charge that it followed, not from a fear of Communism, but from the nature of Christianity and fear for "the values of European civilization"; he compares it to "the case of the Cathers".

But there is a seeming equivocation; Mr. Rubenstein earlier had expressed shock at "The contrast between the liberal faith in enlightenment . . . and the gruesome history of the 20th century . . . " So the question becomes, did the Holocaust arise out of a perceived need for "civilization . . . to defend . . . its inheritance", or on the other hand was the Holocaust "fallout from the catastrophic drop into the barbarism "of the 20th century from "the liberal faith in enlightenment"?

The question of the Holocaust is a part of a far greater evil, greater even than genocide. It is a rational and cognizable element of totalitarianism, *total inhumanness*. People are replaceable; the concept of a human society with freedom in self-government, and rising up in a culture as progress, may very well not be. It is already maligned and excluded from leading universities and schools, from media and entertainment, from government policy, and even often unsupported in our churches. The necessary un-truth to justify the taught hatred, begins with the forced perception that the hate was learned from Christians, but the Enlighteners cursed all religion, both Christian and Jewish; socialism was an offspring of the Enlightenment. Voltaire is noted for his rabid anti-Semitism; and the philosopher of the Enlightenment, Johann Fichte, who helped lay the theoretical foundation for socialism, insisted that "Jews should not be granted civil rights."(40)

Michael Novak recently released information, previously largely kept from the public, that the British Foreign Office contains records revealing "that Pius XII was *early on* (e.a.) willing to risk the entire papacy as a mediator between British and key German generals conspiring against Hitler to seek peace."(41) Actually it came in late 1940; Rudolf Hess's flight to bring peace was on May 10, 1941. Gen. Wedemeyer wrote of peace feelers coming out of Switzerland as late as 1943.

The significance of this has been kept well hidden, as well as the facts. Why did neither Roosevelt nor Churchill (nor any Jewish leaders!) try to follow up even one of these leads? It was widely recognized -- though only occasionally mentioned at the time -- that joining with Stalin was at best a "a gargantuan jest", which started and ended in disgrace indistinguishable from treason. Settlement with Germany, with destruction of the National Socialist Party, would have been brought a united Europe against totalitarianism. There would have been little destruction of Western civilization, an end to totalitarianism, no Holocaust, no Cold War-Korea-Vietnam-Cuba,, no McCarthy, no Watergate, no Clinton. Why was Rudolf Hess ("He came to us of . . . the quality of an envoy": W. Churchill) imprisoned, in solitary confinement, denied any reading material concerning Germany, and apparently eventually murdered. Why was even his wife arrested? Why has not one of the many Holocaust investigators asked, why?.

The refusal to join with powerful German forces to uproot Nazism was by no means an oversight, and it is and must be recognized as an immediate cause of the Holocaust. The effective cause arose from history, from Marx's teaching of hatred for capitalists, which he declared to be a "Judaistic manifestations".(42)

It was Machiavelli who clarified and made precise a growing zeal of intellectuals to grasp total power from what they perceived as the failing motivation of Christian churches. Reject the Christian ethic of gentleness, love, humility and peace, and of the Roman (pagan) virility, manhood, courage, and intelligence. Everything in the state; the ends justifies the means.

All the varied movements, from Machiavelli to the Enlighteners: Voltaire, Diderot, Fichte, and Condorcet; the Economists of 1755 France who first described the total state; the early ideal socialists such as Saint-Simon and his secretary Comte, on to the hard socialists Marx and Lassalle, Moses Hess, Edouard Drumont (all Jews), along with Fourier, Blanqui, Engels, Alphonse Toussenel, and others, down to Nietzsche, Lenin, and Hitler all demanded that control be wrested from religion, and given (as total control) to the State. Even Hegel who valued religion more than many Christians, still would make the State supreme, and therefor total.

Without the Versailles Treaty (1919), there could have been no Hitler; without Communism and "the Jewish radicals he could never have come to power". Communists supported him as "their stalking horse"! Genocide was established as a legitimate socialist tool in the Soviet; the most recent and inhumanly barbaric in Cambodia which the *New York Times* and Anthony Lewis defended as "a vision of a new society", was created by French educated intellectuals. Read moderate Paul Johnson on this, and of Jews of Weimar, in his *Modern Times*.

"ON THE JEWISH QUESTION"

Western civilization faces two momentous threats. First is an internal slide into the inhummaness of Statism; the other is the rising threat from the East. People from Beirut to Beijing view us (the We of New York and Hollywood) as depraved, as a threat, even as hateful. A confrontation in the coming decades with China is inevitable. The internal threat to our human society is most serious, but if overcome, we can confront the East in peace and strength.

The internal attacks began centuries ago, but only in the past century did they lead to appreciable destruction of essential social institutions, albeit still subversively. The movement was essentially totalitarian, in that there was little or no effective organized resistance. Social leaders, in government or business, and in education and even in religion, either joined in the ravaging or were intimidated into inaction, except for some profuse complaining.

The great importance of Christianity to Western civilization was that the churches traditionally provided the essential organized resistance to inhumanness. While "religion" was the object of early attacks on society, it did not really come under specific and open assault, widely and by the whole liberal regime, until 1963 when "a German playwright named Rolf Hochhuth" presented his play, "The Deputy". It is written that this screed of hate, almost overnight transformed Pope Pius XII, and Christianity of which he was a major leader, from "a courageous antagonist of Nazism, a benefactor of war victims . . . and a leader in efforts on behalf of Jewish civilians", recognized and thanked by Golda Meir, Einstein, President Eisenhower and the Jewish Committee, into "the protagonist of a black legend", eventually to "Hitler's Deputy".(1)

Common sense tells us that it did nothing of the kind; merely the We of New York and Hollywood forces the perception. This minor German docu-drama lacked factual support, and was backed by no important studies and evaluation. The momentous, Manichaean transformation was actually but part of the *Liberal Project* started in 1959, which set in motion in "the Sixties" a vast barrage of charges and attacks: America as evil, the flower generation, the lie of "loyal Japanese internment", Wilhelm Reich's and the Jewish Frankfurt School's sex revolution, black radicalism, the ADL's fictitious "Judeo-Christian heritage", attacks on immigration control, on the Constitution, religion and on human society, and most lasting "The Holocaust."

A consideration of "The Holocaust" can properly begin by noting only Jewish claims, and the numerous discussions among Jews and the often vehement diatribes within American Judaism, concerning the nature, cause, even the existence of a particularly planned "Holocaust". Michael Novak of the American Enterprise Institute branded the accusations of Hochhuth and later of John Cornwell as "grossly inflammatory and absurd".(2) Widely recognized authorities, such as Princeton's distinguished historian of diplomacy, Arno Mayer, have denied an organized intent.(3) Holocauster Raul Hilberg declared under oath, "There is no scientific report that shows gas chambers . . . no autopsy". Noam Chomsky jeered "The Holocaust" as a "Zionist hoax". Surviving Jew Aleksandras Shtromas wrote a detailed and moderate account of his experience in the horror, and of his subsequent studies. He concluded that Jews were "not faultless and powerless victims"; "Communism was a Jewish cause", and the "final solution" was a "secret policy . . . kept from the German people" and often implemented by Jewish help.(4)

There are other claims. "After the Bolshevik Revolution, the Jewish presence became intolerable to European religious and political elites who regarded Bolshevism as a Jewish assault on Christianity;" wrote Richard Rubenstein.(5) "Jews are unwilling to acknowledge the challenge they posed to Christianity . . . mortal enemies . . . Marx and Freud seen . . . as a continuation of the rabbinic assault on Christianity".(6) "The most distinctive role of Jews . . . is working to overthrow Christian (Western) civilization . . . ", charged Dennis Prager.(7) "A.S. Lindemann author of *Esau's Tears*, with Hannah Arendt, Jacob Katz, and others, does not accept the comforting but fallacious notion that Jews had nothing to do with the generation of anti-Semitism."(8) The American Jewish Committee was a prime mover in the Liberal Project, a "white holocaust" of civilization.

"Any religious influence in Christian America impinged upon the first-class status of Jews", announced Leo Pfeffer, the architect of "the naked public square" and propagandist who forced a false Constitutional separation of Church and State. After convincing the Supreme Court to ignore the *first right* in the First Amendment and to ban religion from public observance, he got up and crowed that he won because "there was no one on the other side". Then he convinced leftist Catholics to print his hatred for Catholics in their *Commonweal*. "Jewish animus against Catholics" stretches from their defeat of the Catholic supported "Hollywood production code", to Billy Crystal's jokes about the Pope, and the Jewish war to oust a Catholic voice from public discourse. Rabbi S. Dresner noted that Jews had "moved to the forefront of . . . the war on families and morals . . . to the point where they (Jews) are now threatened with extinction," along with the entire country, and West.(9) After nine pages of disparaging Christianity, Dr. A.M. Gessman proclaimed "A Judeo-Christian heritage . . . does not exist",(10). "The Jewish-Christian tradition . . . a Christian fantasy", Rabbi E. Berkovitz.(11) Dershowitzian "Chutzpah" equated the "poisonous secretion" of "friendly Christians" with "Nazi rape". "Our most powerful weapon is racial tension . . . inflaming the negro against Whites . . . instill in Whites a guilt complex . . . ", Israel Cohen.(12)

   R.L. Rubenstein in his *After Auschwitz*(13) left the question hanging; was Christian belief in a Jewish assault (either in pre-war Germany or today's America) justified, and did "The Holocaust" follow from it? Holocaust theologians and dominating shouts deny a Jewish or Communist assault, blaming Christianity and Western civilization. Did the Holocaust arise from a need of Western "civilization to defend . . . its inheritance", or from a drop into the barbarism "of the 20th century"? There is, of course, not one bit of evidence that even suggests that any segment of civilization, religious or secular, ever sought to defend itself with the Holocaust.

   David Novak gives a moderate and reasonable analysis. "Modern secularism, with its explicit denial of any normative transcendence, is a far more immediate condition encouraging Nazi nihilism, than Christian ambivalence about Jews. Nazism is . . . not a simple extension of even medieval Christian-anti-Judaism. Contemporary Jewish opposition to Christianity, supposedly coming from the Holocaust, implies a favorable judgment of secularism rather than . . . (as cause for) removal of a normative transcendence . . . that created the spiritual vacuum . . . which both Nazism and Communism rushed to fill. Seems to say Jews can relate to (anything) but Christians".(14)

   But even these ideas, cogent as they are, miss completely the central issue, which is not the holocausts. Christianity-and-the-Holocaust is not the problem. Christianity and Western civilization are but organs of human society, and *it* is what must be destroyed for the ascension of the intellectual's total regime. All of the holocausts of the 20th Century constitute but an extension of the long struggle of intellectuals to destroy organized human society for the ascension of their total regime. A Jewish "Holocaust" has been admittedly "politically useful" in obscuring that struggle and the Jewish part in it. The naked totalitarian power that still ravages humanness around the world is the real horror. "The Holocaust" has served as a highly charged shield preventing examination of the true evil, or even minor social comment on it.

Without Franklin Roosevelt's support of Communism, followed by its establishment in the "mainstream" of the 50s and 60s, Hochhuth would have remained unknown. A "Holocaust Cult" is said to have replaced Judasim and "Jewish fear became politically useful . . . tolerant rational elements in Jewish life was overwhelmed by rage and worship of power", so wrote Leon Wieseltier.(15)   Even the Anti-Defamation League, in response to "The Deputy", formally declared that action by Pius "would have provoked the Nazis to brutal retaliation . . ."(16)   Kevin Madigan noted "the post-war chorus of praise (for Pius XII) . . . Golda Meir, Eisenhower, Einstein",(17) and declared the writings of Hochhuth, and more recently of John Cornwell excoriating the Pope were "grossly defamatory and absurd".(18)

The disaster of 9-11 has produced only momentarily perhaps a great awakening in many people, particularly among liberal leaders. By moving quickly this can be taken advantage of as an incentive to rebuild a human society. The Greeks founded the basic culture of civilization as a means for gathering their strength in the face of encroachments from the East; we must also in order to become strong enough to face the East in peace with confidence. Statism gradually debilitates and can be seen as doing so. Use the reason that Reasoners, Enlighteners, and liberals trusted so highly, but misused, in service of a supreme purpose, to save the goal of three thousand years of struggle and the civilization which it produced.

Recovery of a human society requires rebuilding families. We may define as generalized pauperization, with Jacob Riis, anything that degrades people, robbing them of human attributes and destroying respect for themselves and responsibility for social humanness.(19)   Family-destructive behaviorisms are not diseases, nor rights, but things to be taught as contemptible and stamped out.

The current madness that the State cannot protect society from terrorism; it is but an excuse for total control. Our original Constitutional social-contract must be reaffirmed. The 14th Amendment is said to have repealed the Constitutional intent that "all that pertains to the lives, liberties and properties of the people" is the sole concern of the people in there local governments. But it was never adopted legally, and in any case was ruled as concerning only Civil War issues. Renegades who would claim otherwise must be repudiated and dismissed. Education in humanness and self government must explicate and celebrate humanness as a purpose, central to religion; all institutions of society should be controlled by society; *education must no more be controlled by the State than is religion.*

We come again to immigration, the lies about which are as monumentous as is its importance to renegades seeking to destroy society. They claim, for example, that aliens are needed to fill the lowest paid jobs, when the truth is obvious that those jobs wouldn't be low paid were it not for the availability of illegal immigrants. More aliens entered America in the Seventies than in any previous time in history. Those who attack families and force lower birthrates are identical to those who claim we need more people. We must go back to raising our own children, for our own salvation and the salvation of Western civilization. We must begin training aliens that are here as a result of illegal acts, in specialties needed in their home country and in human society, and return them there to create in their homelands their own cultures.

Finally we must begin by teaching the greatness of human society, and build new media institutions to facilitate it. Begin with current institutions, expanding and strengthening with growth. Equally important is getting children out of State public-schools.

Today our "mainstream" is controlled through money and through intimidation, largely by Jews. Liberals and radicals led by Jews, have destroyed our music, art, religion, Constitution and laws, and our social structure. The figures are staggering, Jews as "players not victims": 26 percent of top media core, 60 percent of Hollywood, 40 percent of top law officers, 16 of top 40 of Forbes 400, besides nearly total control of foundations, unions, and much even of the Christian hierarchy. So declared Philip Weiss in *New York* magazine. Jews have nominal control (because even when small in number, they are organized and have money and influence, and can coerce the support of the entire regime) of books and magazine publishing (name one major magazine of opinion not a Jewish house-organ or firmly controlled as "mainstream"), of representation on all important boards and commissions: scientific, law, health, cultural, education, and unions. Nearly every TV consultant on law, science, social problems, or politics is a Jew, or of a Jewish organization. Rabbi Irving Greenberg declared truculently, "Jews owe nothing to Christianity." "Anyone . . . believing that tolerance is a Jewish virtue will be in for a surprise," J.P. Stern.(20)

I know of no more shameful grovelling subordination by a people in the entire history of the world than that of acquiescing to a great "finger of shame" constructed on the Mall of the American People: "The Holocaust" memorial. We have been blamed for not coming soon enough; we had no intention of coming, and did so only due to FDR's trick. But he is the one who had the opportunity to receive massive German help in ousting Hitler and the Nazi party -- more than once, and certainly Jews knew of it -- and both totally ignored it. Then there is the malignant slander: "the guilt of every Christian . . . (for) complicity, indeed causation, of the murder of Jews", by Rabbi Berkovitz.

There can be no real doubt but that modern anti-Semitism was a product of socialists, including Jewish socialists, which they received from the liberal Enlighteners. Holocaust theologians' avoidance of the very idea of a socialist origin is similar to Red Cronkite spending an hour discussing Orwell's *1984* without once mentioning Communism. Philip Gourevitch, editor of *Forward*, claimed a "proper dose of Holocaust will provide Jews protection from murder by the U.S." and he was not pleased that the Holocaust Museum "let America off too easily." "Jewish hatred of Christians in Russia", wrote R. Rubinstein, "helped bring death to millions of people including tens of thousands of priests". "When I hear Christian America, I see barbed wire," a Rabbi.(21)

Every people "strives to . . . transmit to present and coming generations the spiritual labor of the race. *It is not* a matter of indifference who writes the Christmas articles (or music) . . . (or) how the young are educated in their own spirit . . . " so wrote Rabbi Dr. Manfred Reifer in 1933. "We played with their most holy possessions . . . and made fun of all that was sacred to the nation . . . We made revolutions . . . roused passions . . . The Jews: Marx declared war on capitalism, Lassalle organized the masses . . . Eduard Bernstein popularized ideology . . . Liebknecht and Luxemburg called the Spartacist movement . . . Kurt Eisner the Bavarian Soviet (and Bela Kun the Hungarian Soviet) . . . These uprooted persons . . . imagined they possessed the power to transplant the ideas of Isaiah into the alleys of Germany, to storm Valhalla with Amos. At times they succeeded . . . but they bury the Jewish people under the ruins of a world that has collapsed".(22) So the holocaust! A similar article was written in America by Marcus Eli Ravage, in *The Century*, 5,2, 1928. That was over 70 years ago; we now all have an opportunity to correct our paths.

Paul Johnson presented an invaluable account of the 20th Century in his *Modern Times*. In his chapter "Waiting for Hitler", he spelled it out. "There is nothing more galling than a cultural tyranny". Weimar made "modern" a decadent *Kalturbolschewismus: The Blue Angel,* themes of homosexuality, sadomasochism, transvestism and incest. Sexual freedoms and pacifism were exalted while the German, the army, state, universities, the Church and especially the middle class were savaged and ridiculed. Jewish Kurt Tucholsky a gifted satirist, declared "no secret of the German Army I would not give readily to an enemy". "He intended to arouse hatred. He succeeded".(23)

In further testimony on the "unrivaled influences" of Jews since WW II see B. Ginsberg, *The Fatal Embrace,* 1993; E.S. Shapiro, *Time for Healing,* 1992; C. Silverman, *A Certain People,* 1985; J.J. Goldberg, *Jewish Power,* 1996, and N. F. Cantor, *The Sacred Chain,* 1994.

"They claimed they were the German *Geist* . . . represented Germany . . . spoke in its name . . . They sat in the front row . . . awarded themselves knighthoods . . . what they did not permit did not exist . . . who ever served them was sure to succeed . . . appeared on stages . . . in their journals, was recommended whether . . . rights or bolshevism . . . rotten Negro music or dancing nude . . . There never was a more impudent dictatorship".(23) So too in Clinton's America.

The film directors were Jewish . . . half the playwrights, they were dominant in light entertainment and theater criticism. Jews owned important newspapers, ran the influential art galleries . . . were strong in publishing, in big department stores. "A Jewish cultural conspiracy seemed plausible", in Weimar and Clinton's America. We now have time to cooperate and to rebuild Western Civilization. It will not likely come again. The disaster of 9-11 may have provided the consciousness raising need to loosen people for action.

Begin by structuring an entirely new and independent media, while developing, consolidating, and organizing what exists, develop a non-state education, reassert our Founder's Constitution, and regain a culture for human society. By not opposing or attacking anyone, but simply in rebuilding our human institutions there can be no legitimate objection of any kind. We can in fact demand support from all.

Ask all to participate, with the understanding that the goal is a human society on the basis of Western civilization and self government -- with no compromises. Jews cannot afford not to join, for certainly they will survive or fall with civilization. Begin by removing the "finger of shame" from our nation's Mall. How shameful. In place of their false memorial, the Jews should create an institution for the study of guidance for human societies in recognizing and avoiding totalitarianism. Cancel a proposed M.L. King memorial. King was no friend to America, to Christianity, or to human society; he plagiarized his doctoral thesis, and his degree was revoked; he plagiarized his famous dream speech; he preached at a meeting in Chicago while thugs with bongo drums chanted "Kill Whitey!" "Kill Whitey!" And he declared at New York's Riverside Church that America killed a million children in Vietnam, in return for millions of dollars of Soviet money. Last year at the local library on Feb. 12, a whole wall was dedicated to King; not one note of Lincoln. Black people should renew the work of Booker T. Washington in creating independent black leaders.

Note Added: Lenin explained that the article written by Karl Marx in 1844, entitled "On the Jewish Question", one of the most bigoted attacks against the Jewish community ever published, marked "Marx's transition from (socialist) idealism to hard Communism". Marx and generally all socialists taught a vigorous antisemitism which they received from the Enlighteners, and an Aryan superiority as a means of attracting followers. Hitler supported all three: Aryan superiority, antisemitism, and socialism, but only the former was tarred with Nazism.

X ON GUIDANCE

"To have his path made clear to him is the aspiration of every human being." But one must have a directing purpose before selecting a particular path. That direction was always taken as a given and understood until the last century; the goal was to be a human being, as *fixed* by God or Nature.

Primitive man had advanced to a high level of humanness as evidenced incontrovertibly by the quality of his Paleolithic art. His miraculous progress was due to guidance by a supreme, externally imposed purpose to enhance his survival, which had been driving him, raising him up in humanness. While survival reigned as the supreme social purpose, leaders and people had been bound together tightly, as on a frail craft in which they had to cooperate in order to stay afloat. However, when reasoned advances in the physical world greatly reduced the threat to their survival, it was like reaching dry ground. Suddenly shrewd individuals realized that they had been released from their social bonds and could seek their own advancement.

But where to? All human activity depends upon guidance. Men are directed by feelings but actions must be reasoned, which in turn depends upon what is known. Modern irrationality is nowhere better exemplified than in demands to "do our own thing" and to reject standards. Nonsense. (It is obvious whom they follow.) Go ahead, do your own thing, ignore a red light; but 2-2 will still equal 0. Primitive men received their guidance from feelings, "forces", according to Durkheim, which arose from their society, which were "kindred and from the outside". He explained their "fantastic beliefs and barbaric rites" as erring responses to real forces.

So when the force for survival faded and traditional guidance was gone, what were ancient intellectuals to do; they had no knowledge of such a calamity. But as chaos mounted it was obvious that social order had to be regained. Details are unknown, but we know what happened; eventually intellectuals were able to terrorize the people with threats of "angry gods" and other superstition, into a sub human servitude. It was the great contribution of the Greeks to develop a new self-imposed purpose, for social guidance and rationality, rejecting "Seers who bring terror to keep men afraid." The Christian world followed with an organization to explicate and celebrate its human purpose.

Religion is the last thing that many people want to talk about, principally because they have no understanding of what it is, and what they have been told is largely untrue. Little recognition is given, even by Christian theologians, to the dichotomy involved. On one hand the word "religion" is a relatively new word for a very old concept: man's spiritual world of feelings, to rise up, and to which he gave that name which opened to him as a result of a long struggle. On the other hand the perception is forced that religion is that corruption of the ancient tyrannies that enslaved our ancestors.

In recent centuries intellectuals have again attempted to coerce people into a total regime, while damning the religion that had structured Western civilization as superstitions and priestly impositions for social control, and equating it to the ancient god-king priesthoods. As a nearly lone objector, Hegel countered by declaring it "absurd to maintain that priests thought up religion as a fraud for their own benefit . . . " However, Hegel misunderstood. That was exactly the *intent* of *both* the ancient intellectual priesthoods and again of the evil deceptions of recent intellectuals in calumnizing Christianity. They have had a number of opportunities to demonstrate their own promises, one lasting some 70 years, with each case ending in disaster much like the ancient tyrannies.

The superstructure of Christianity does contain relics from ancient god-king empires, such as King Solomon and his thousand wives, and also an assortment of claims that had circulated in the Middle East for centuries in the Roman Empire: from Egypt the Trinity, a Last Supper, immortality and adoration of Mother and Child, from elsewhere a resurrection, millenarianism, a duality of God-Satan, and the eucharist. However, Judaism exchanged its kings for lawgivers, while Christian philosophy was from the beginning soundly based on concepts from the Greeks: "There is a divinity in man", which seeks that proper to human beings.

As for theological claims, consider a Creation; the origin of the universe is totally unaccountable in any known physical science, and a Creation is the only alternative to an "always here" which raises more problems. As for prophets and revelations, most people at some time feel that they have been moved by an unknown power. Beyond that, we know that it is very difficult to induce the masses of people to continue the struggle for humanness. My God, look at today! When the effort is for upholding a human society, why not allow a little slack, a small part of that allowed to intellectuals in pushing their evil ideologies?

Life is a bridge that takes us through a time to be, from one infinity to another. It is a bridge deftly constructed with guidance and support for humanness. Over the edges, which are clearly marked, sinks inhumanness. The threat of 9-11, largely a failure of government, is being used to push us off, into the iron arms of the State. People can and will be safe and free only if they are organized to protect themselves. Samuel Johnson explained that "words are signs of ideas". And he found words which he labeled as "absurdities" in Dryden, whom he claimed "delighted to tread upon the brink of meaning". As an example: "upon our orb's last verge we go, and see the ocean hanging on the sky . . ." An obvious space view; Dryden could imagine way out there in the blue, "From thence . . . on the lunar world securely pry".

Let us then imagine our own vision of that "orb", as of all taking part, especially the young people, in rebuilding a world "proper to man and God". Don't be frightened of humanness, or of religion. Those who damn all efforts toward either must be recognized as renegades seeking to crush all humanity into a technologically advanced inhumanness.

There are many however who reject religion out of misunderstanding or on the basis of specific claims, who nevertheless wish, and will work, to retain human society. Accept them; as seekers of human society they make possible any and all religion. Likewise humanists should accept the religious, as providing a more strongly motivated core opposing an obvious inhuman tyranny.

Marxist Terry Eagleton bragged "There's a tremendous prize out there, and we're the only players in the arena". All of Western civilization must get in the spirit of rebuilding and make a real game of it, a new Insaturation. It is a central aim of this book to induce all people, particularly young people to get back in the game. Most of the West is currently in a state of affluent indifference to the surrounding reality, and of Durkheim's anomie or rulelessness.(1) Today people are "put-off" by religion, by even humanness, but are unconcerned by the corruption, rot, and evil all about them and in the "regime".

Irrationality and collateral lies rule all. "Most disastrous . . . by no means (is it) . . . that groups have abandoned themselves to irrationalism. Far worse . . . other groups from whom we had expected some resistance . . . have lost their belief in the powers of reason". So wrote the scholar Karl Mannheim in his *Man and Society* over 60 years ago.(2) He included an extended discussion of what he meant by "rational". Not the common rationalism, as an exaggerated faith in the technical and scientific; rather as behavior which results when a series of actions is organized in such a way that they lead to a previously defined goal.

I would limit it to a defined human goal, for an inhuman goal cannot truly be rational for a human being on teleonomic (species preserving) grounds. Most of the secular goals of modernity have not been intended to be human: equality, social justice, democracy, liberalism, feminism, and even "peace" were planned invariably, by the regime, to be destructive of human society. On the other hand religion, according to Hegel, "Reason's highest and most rational work", commonly and particularly Christianity was a perfecter, or even creator, of most that we claim to characterize humanness.

First, is to begin !! Begin discussions of human society, even as you work to recreate human social institutions, avoiding all distractions.

Learn of and discuss the efforts by the regime and by public education, foundations, and minorities, that are destructive of civilization, humanness, and a self-governing society. Bureaucrats make grants of millions of dollars of tax money to radical groups seeking to destroy rational public policies by stoking irrational fears and inflaming hatreds. Renegade groups are awarded million-dollar grants to challenge governmental environmental policies in court; to lawyer groups instituting billion dollar lawsuits on the narrowest of claims in corrupt courts; to educationalist lobbyist-renegades working to destroy long held moral rules and social customs. Foundations and even corporations have financed illegal immigration, Constitutional challenges to human rights, sexual perverts such as Wilhelm Reich and Alfred Kinsey, and now to a range of homosexual renegades forcing their teachings into public schools, on and on. Become familiar with current assaults on human society, often financed by tax or tax-exempt foundation money. All firmly supported by the mainstream.

Learn about these activities for background assurance, for motivation, but don't waste time opposing them. Rather work to build by-passes around them; then cut them off with political and economic boycotts. And always seek to gather others.

NOTE ON RELIGION

There is some in science which is denied by other scientists. In the past certain things were believed which later were proven to be untrue or only partially true. Human endeavors covered by the modern word "religion" are older and broader than much science. What is today known as religion began as man's erring attempts to comprehend the human condition in his society, and to provide teachings, guidance, and celebrations of "forces" felt to be kindred and helpful. These "forces" the Greeks took as evidence for "a divinity in man". Whether the divinity is in man as placed there by God, or is in God Himself, or whether it arises from man's society as a gift of his Maker, is important only in the accommodations.

J.S. Mill wrote that "The most incessant occupation (of man) . . . is the ascertainment of the truth." Therein lies a great problem: over the past millennia there has been the truth proclaimed by Christian teachers; a very different truth has come from intellectuals seeking to destroy religion, to facilitate coercing all people into a Statism. In fact, liberal J.S. Mill complained that the power of religion came not as much from itself as "from its control over public opinion -- of the truth". Whom do you suppose Mill believed should control public opinion? Compare the human progress under Christian guidance to that provided by secular intellectuals.

Natural law, families, and parental tenderness, education in social behavior, and culture are all innate, base, they began evolving long before conscious reason, ideas, and religion and science. In fact religion and science arose out of conscious man's fascination concerning the nature of experienced innate "forces" or feelings, and the relationship of all of these to his clan, his society; so came totemism, the root of all major religions; the Great Spirit was an expression for the forces man felt from his society. Secular intellectuals teach people that there is no such thing as a given human nature, even as they recognize a dog's or a cat's innateness. They teach that families, morality, culture, and religion, all of which evolved under innate forces, are but impositions, coerced along with superstitions. They work not only to obscure families of man and wife and their children as the greatest source of happiness, hope, and comfort in human life; they seek to arrange for their impossibility. Likewise they work to destroy all supporting institutions and the very existence of organized society, corroding all human attachments in a flood of aliens, promiscuities, and brutishness. Such is the record of modern secular regimes. The ancient tyrannies subverted true religion with superstitions for "social control". Today's intellectual struggle to destroy religion and all humanness, in order to gain total control; they attempt to stigmatize all religion as superstitions.

The essential function of religion is as social guidance in humanness, and support for families, for children, women, social decencies, education, and morality. All of the greatest art, literature, and music of Western civilization has been produced by people educated as Christians, been supported by Christian churches, and celebrated as great human achievements in teaching people to rise up.

Intense opposition arose in the famous seventeenth century between science and religion. Some two millennia earlier the Greeks had proposed a spherical earth, along with other celestial bodies, even calculating -- quite well -- the diameter of the earth. Copernicus, as the fifteenth century was ending, urged the "hypothesis" of heliocentricity. Early in the 1600s Galileo had perfected his new telescope, permitting him to observe the rotation of moons around Jupiter and the phases of Venus. These observations, along with other facts concerning tidal motion, he determined to be explainable only on a Copernican, heliocentric model of the universe. Since the whole of Christian theology, advanced since the time of Christ, was based in an assumption that man on his Earth was the center of God's Creation and concern; reducing him to a mere cosmic speck was totally anathemic to theologians, although at one stage Galileo held the Pope's interest. You know the rest of the story, and for nearly 150 years after Copernicus had centered our universe on the sun, very few of even the well education people accepted heliocentricity. Then Bernard de Fontenelle a man of infinite decency, as a missionary of science wrote his *Plurality of Worlds*. He imagined six evenings of conversations, in a garden under the stars, with a beautiful and intelligent marquese. Through the multitude of stars the allure of her beauty is felt as he tells her that the sun is but the closest star and its planets little rotating spheres. The moon and other planets might also be inhabited, he suggested, by beings with other senses. Would they see the truth as we do, or might truth be relative? Fontenelle saved the situation by emphasizing the great beauty and order to the universe; comparing it to a watch, he insisted only a divine power of supreme intelligence could have been the Creator.

This vastly more marvelous Creation could not be taken as an affront to the Church. Quite soon man's new heliocentric abode was widely accepted. To believe that "all of Christ's promises," and all of man's spiritual world should be dashed because of discovered errors in primitive concepts shows little real belief.

Whether our universe was Created, created by Nature's chance, or was "always here", its existence is not a part of any natural science; hence it is by definition, supernatural. Similarly we have no way of knowing whether life originated with God or Nature's chance, but an "operational reason", which facilitated both the absorption of information from the environment and the enactment of a response according to site-specific data, inserted into all life *ab initio* with a will to survive and to rise up, seems a double infinity beyond a mutational accomplishment.

Religious people often reject comparisons between man and animals, but there is no reason to believe that God does. Their concern is proper but misplaced; all life has many things in common, whether from God or Nature, and one need not fear comparisons; they are often revealing. But a major continuing issue concerns whether man has an objective nature at all, whether determined by God or Nature. In a sense, this is a fundamental existential question of all religion, and of science, assuming that it is this endowed nature that will bring to man the greatest humanness. It seems unquestionably true that much animal behavior prefigures human behavior, as that of the child prefigures the man. What we see distinctly and repeatedly in animals is often innate also in man, from the Maker. All social animals exhibit powerful innate restraints on behavior similar to natural law, morality and charity; there is evidence that these are phylogenetic adaptations in man, not mere cultural "values", changeable as styles.

Galileo "adduced ironically" that the tides could not be used to show the motion of the earth, "without limiting God's omniscience". Today many people spend considerable time in claiming that "the facts of evolution" cannot be accepted as presenting God's mode of Creation without similarly limiting His omniscience or reducing man to an animal. The fact is that God's gift of reason has permitted man to rise to a humanness that is ultimately beyond his animal childhood, as Copernicus and Galileo presented a far more miraculous universe. The real problem lies neither with the conservative theologians nor the advancing scientists; it is liberal intellectuals who seek to stigmatize and spread contempt and even hate with such monstrosities as Darwinian sociology, lies about the Scopes Trial (in Tenn.), Margaret Mead's sexology, and university renegades who continue to trick people out of their common senses.

It is another liberal deceit to present the choice as between "reason" and superstitions. Clearly the rational-secular choice is between striving to rise up in humanness, after the Greeks, and on the other hand an indifference to inhumanness. Man's adventures in inhumanness have in modernity (and, post-mod.) only begun. I urge anyone interested in pursuing the subject to examine the disgusting, abhorrent forms of parasitism that have evolved in the animal life of insects; clientism to the State could produce unimaginable corruption.

Rebuilding must begin by organizing cells for discussions, by all persons who can be induced to do so, of the need for an organized human society, which can and will teach and lead people to comprehend that without such a vigilant organization they are certain to be coaxed and forced into inhuman activity and eventually into a sub-human servitude.

A profound comprehension of society, culture, and rationality are essential for the vigorous motivation to protect and to maintain human society.

REFERENCES

CHAPTER II THE WAR

1. Dawidowicz, Lucy, *The New Leader*, 12,22, 1952.

2. Lyons, Eugene, *The Red Decade*, 1941, p. 324-340.

3. See "Introduction" to Vantage Edition and Authors Notes to *The Rosenberg File* by R. Radosh and J. Milton, 1984, and the Introduction by David Horowitz to S.S. Powell's *Covert Cadre*, 1987.

4. Lorenz, Konrad, *Behind The Mirror*, 1973, p. 206.

CHAPTER III THE DEMONIC DREAM

1. Tocqueville, Alexis de, *L' Ancien regime*, Gilbert translation, p. 162-164.

2. "Generation X", *Atlantic Monthly*, 11, 1999, p.8.

3. Sandel, M.J., *Atlantic Monthly*, 3, 1996, p. 57.

4. Mannheim, Karl, *Man and Society*, p. 39-75, and translator's "Introduction" by Edward Shils, Harcourt, Brace and Co. (1940).

CHAPTER IV   THE SUPREME QUESTION

1. Bloom, Allen, *Giants*, 1990, p. 277.
2. Chambers, Whittaker, *Witness*, 1952, p. 9.
3. Van Doren Stern, Philip, *Prehistoric Europe*, 1969, p. 162.
4. Leakey, Richard, *The Origin of Humankind*, 1994, p. 104.
5. Tocqueville, Alexis de: *Democracy in America*, Vol. II, 1840, p. 320-21.   (Fourth Book, Chapt. VI).
6. Schweitzer, Albert, *The Philosophy of Civilization*, 1923, Translated 1949, p. 9.
7. Lippmann, Walter, *The Good Society*, 1936, p. 4.
8. Ward, Barbara, *Policy for the West*, 1951.
9. Mill, John Stuart, The *Philosophy of J.S. Mills*, Ed. M. Cohen, 1961, p. 501.
10. Mill, John Stuart, Delivered at the University of St. Andrews, Feb. 1, 1867; *Dissertations and Discussions*, 1875, Vol. IV., p. 332-402.
11. Weber, Max, *Protestant Ethic*, Translated by Talcott Parsons, 1930, p. 13.
12. Lorenz, Konrad, *Behind the Mirror*, 1973,   p. 182.
13. Barfield, Owen, *History in English Words*, Chapt. 1, and others.
14. Ceaser, J.M., *Reconstructing America*, 1997.   Also Baudrillard, J., *Amérique*, 1986.

NOTE ON ARYANS

1. Barfield, Owen, *History in English Words*, 1953.

2. Childe, V. Gordon, *The Aryans*, 1987.

3. Mariner, Joanne, *No Escape: Male Rape in U.S. Prisons*, Human Rights Watch, 2001. See also *Culture Wars*, 4, 00, p. 32.

CHAPTER V HUMANNESS

1. Coon, Carleton S., *The Story of Man*, 1962, P.9.

2. Mill, John Stuart, Delivered at the University of St. Andrews, Feb. 1, 1867; *Dissertation and Discussions*, 1875, Vol. IV., p. 332-402.

3A. It is a biological law that new species evolve rapidly, but soon stabilize. Once a critical genetic breakthrough is attained, "local adjustments" may accomplish much of the rapid evolution, with stabilization when complete. Accordingly man evolved as a hunter, nearly solely in nature; today he is most productive when organized as to give full expression to those capacities developed as a hunter. It is seldom realized that teaching babies to walk began some 10 million years ago, collaterally with society and our forebears career as hunter. Writers refer to human bipedelism as evolved innateness; necessary physiological adaptations of course are. But the baby "animal" must be taught how. Note the difference: wasp nest-building is also innate, but does not need to be taught.

3. Lorenz, Konrad, *Behind the Mirror*, 1973, p. 182.

4. Durkheim, Emile, *Elementary Forms of Religious Life*, 1915, p. 9-13.

5. Stern, P. Van Doren, *Prehistoric Europe*, 1969, p. 162.

6. Leakey, R., *The Origin of Humankind*, 1994, p. 104.

7. Tocqueville, Alex de, *The Ancient Regime, P.* 162-164.

8. Trilling, Lionel; *Beyond Culture*, 1955, p. 161.

9. Bloom, Allen, *Closing of the American Mind*, 1987, p. 351.

10. Trilling, op cit, p. 147.

11. Paul, *Second Epistle to the Thessalonians*, 3:14,15.

12. Ward, Barbara, *Policy for the West, 1951*.

CHAPTER VI   WWII

1. Schlesinger, A.M., NY *Times Book Rev.*, 5,9,1948.

2. Schlesinger, A.M., *Wall Street Journal*, 6,21,1990.

3. Tully, Grace, *FDR, My Boss*.

3A. Borgquist, Daryl S., *Navel Institute Proceedings, Naval History*, May-June, 1999, "Advance Warning", about Pearl Harbor. See also *The New American*, 7,30,01, p. 44, and 7,2,01, p. 24.

4. Roosevelt, Elliott, *As He Saw It*, 1946, p. 177.

5. Fuller, Maj. Gen. J.F.C., *The Second World War*, 1948.

6. Chambers, Whitaker, *Witness*, 1952, p. 469.

7. Wedemeyer, General A.C., *Reports*, 1958, p. 9. See also, W. Churchill, *The Grand Alliance*, 1950, p. 23-4.

8. Fuller, op. cit.

9. Wedemeyer, op. cit., p. 96; and *Commentary*, 7-8,99, p. 20.

10. Bullitt, George, *Life*, 8,30,1948.

11. Johnson, Paul, *Modern Times*, 1982, p. 345.

12. Ibid., P. 345.

13. Lyons, Eugene, *The Red Decade*, 1941, p. 348-351.

14. Clark, Ronald, *The Man Who Broke Purple*, 1977.

15. Schlesinger, A.M., *New York Times, Book Rev.*, 5,9,1948.

16. Beard, C.A., *President Roosevelt*, 1948.

17. Morgenstern, George, *Pearl Harbor*, 1947.

18. Crocker, G.N., *Roosevelt's Road to Russia*, 1959.

19. Reports of the Army Pearl Harbor Board and the Navy Court of Inquiry, *United States News*, Sept. 1, 1945.

20. Report of the Joint Congressional Committee, U.S. Printing Office, Washington, 1946.

21. Morgenstern, op. cit., p. 64.

22. Lyons, Eugene, *The Red Decade*, 1941, p. 302-307, 393-399.

23. Crocker, op. cit., p. 71.

24. Grew, J.C., Ambassador to Japan, *Ten Years In Japan*, p. 444.

25. Morgenstern, op. cit., p. 151,2.
26. Ibid., p. 153.
27. Ibid., p. 248,9. Also 27A - *Chronicles*, 10,02, p.13.
28. Ibid., p. 385.
29. Ibid., p. 215.
30. Ibid., p. 229.
31. Ibid., p. 267,8.
32. Ibid., p. 398.
33. Ibid., p. 268, 390.
34. Ibid., p. 171,269,270,275.
35. Ibid., p. 275, 276.
36. Ibid., p. 248-278.
37. Ibid., p. 275-277.
38. Ibid., p. 270-271.
39. Ibid., p. 269-270.
40. Ibid., 216,17.
41. Kennan, Geo. F., *Memoirs*, p. 264,5.
42. Johnson, op. cit., 405,5.
43. Lukacs, J.A., *The Great Powers*, p. 655.
44. Roosevelt, F.D., Post-Yalta Radio Address to Congress and Nation, March 1, 1945.

45. Bullitt, W.C., "A Report on China", *Life*, 10,3,1947.

46. Bullitt, W.C., *Reader's Digest*, 6,47.

47. Roosevelt, E., *As He Saw It*, 1946.

48. Deane, Gen. J.R., *The Strange Alliance*, 1947.

49. Romerstein, H. and Brindel, E., *The Verona Secrets*, 2000.

50. Moynihan, D.P., *Academic Questions*, Winter 1996-97, p.31.

51. House Comm. on Un-American Activities, "Hearings on Shipment of Atomic Materials to the Soviets", Dec. 7, 1949, p. 941-957, also 933. See also, Jordan, Major G. R., Diaries.

CHAPTER VII WAR ON HUMAN SOCIETY

1. Blumenfeld, S.L., *NEA: Trojan Horse*, 1985, p. 38-9.

2. Arendt, H., *On Revolution*, 1965, p. 136, 171-2.

3. Morison, S.E., *Oxford History of the American People*, 1965, P. 124.

3A. Trilling, Diana, *The New Republic*, 11,1,93.

4. Hall, G.S., *Life and Confessions*, 1923, p. 223.

5. Dewey, John, *University Record*, I, 1896, p. 417-422; op. cit. Blumenfeld, p. 104.

6. Dewey, J. *Education and the Social Order*, 1934, p. 10.

7. Tyack, David, *Managers of Virtue*, 1982, p. 130.

8. IBID, p. 130.
9. IBID, p. 143.
10. Orton, S.T., *J.Ed. Psychology*, 2, 1929.
11. Gates, A.I. and Bond, G.L., NEA, *Journal*, Oct., 1936.
12. *Life* Magazine, Ap., 1947.
13. Flesch, Rudolf, Dr., *Why Johnny Can't Read, 1955*.
14. Chall, Jeanne, Dr., *Learning to Read*, 1967.
15. International Reading Association, *J. of Reading*, Jan. 1969.
16. Damerell, R.G., *Education's Smoking Gun*, 1985, 280,1, p.A.
17. Connell, D., NEA, *Journal*, 9, 1969.
18. Abel, Jules, *Rockefeller Billions*, 1967.
19. Ravitch, Diana, *A Century of Failed School Reform*, 2000.
20. Wolfe, Alan S., *The New Republic*, 12, 11, 2000, p. 38.
20A. *The New Republic*, 1,22,01, p. 4, from an Ed. Prof.
21. Wagschal, P., *Illiterate With Doctorates*, University of Massachusetts, School of Ed., *Alumni Newsletter*, Feb. 1980, Vol. 5, No. 1, p. 4. Also Damerell, op. cit., P. 73.
22. Damerell, op, cit., p. 21.
23. Lauchner, A.H., *Bulletin*, Nat. Ass'n. Sec. School Principals, March 1951, p. 299, quoted in Mortimer Smith, *The Diminished Mind*, 1969, p. 24.

24. Simon, John, *Paradigm's Lost*, 1980, p. 155.

25. Wagschal, op. cit.

26. Simon, op. cit.

27. *Newsweek*, 10,29,01, p. 68.

28. Wagschal, op. cit.

29. Damerell, op. cit.

30. Auden, W.H., Forward To Owen Barfield's *History in English Words*, 1985 Edition.

31. Coleman Report, *Academic Questions*, P. 90-91.

32. Chubb and Moe Report, Atlantic Monthly, Jan. 1991.

33. *The New Republic*, 9,19,94, p. 14; see also *Harper's* 3,84, p. 22.

34. Coombs, Marian N., *Chronicles*, 11,99, p.45.

35. Powers, R., *The Dilemma of Education in a Democracy*, 1984. See also Sandra Stotsky's excellent and vitally important *Losing Our Language*; reviewed in *Comm.* 5, 99, p. 78.

36. Cohen, Felix, *American Socialist Quarterly*, Nov. 1935, Vol. 4, p. 21.

37. Adams, J.T., *March of Democracy*, II, 1937, p. 70.

38. Lowell, J.R., *Bigelow Papers*.

39. Lincoln, A., *speeches and Writings*, 1832-1858, Library of America, 1984, p. 316.

40. Adams, op. cit., Vol. 1, p. 384.

41. Ibid., p. 403.

42. Ibid., p. 404.

43. Adams, op. cit., Vol 2, p. 70.

44. Flack, Horace, *The Adoption of the Fourteenth Amendment*, 1908.

45. Morison, op. cit., p. 714.

CHAPTER VIII   CONSPIRACY

1. Rabinowitz, Dorothy, *Wall Street Journal*, 12,2,1991.

2. *The New American*, 5,8,2000, p. 35, "Americanist Chairman -- Martin Dies", by Jane H. Ingraham.

3. Lyons, Eugene, *Red Decade*, 1941, particularly, p. 382-386, 391 and p. 394-397.

4. Morison, S.E., *Oxford History of the American People*, 1965, p. 999.

5. Daenecke, J.D., "The America First Committee", *Chronicles*, 12,1991, p. 16. See also an account of J.T. Flynn (a former liberal *New Republic* regular columnist) in the *New American*, 1,31,2000, p. 28.

6. *The Barnes Review*, No./Dec. 1999, p. 5 gives a brief but concise narrative of the trial, including essentially the only references to books or histories on the trial, for example, Ronald Radosh, *Prophets on the Right*, 1975, and David Baxter (a defendant), "The Great Sedition Trial of 1944", *The Journal of Historical Review*, Spring, 1985.

7. Rusher, Wm., *Am. Spectator*, 3,84, p. 2,3.

8. Rieff, D., *The New Republic*, 7,28,86, p. 37.

9. *The New American*, 9,2,1996, p. 36, quoting Robert Amory (presumably one of the guests).

10. Moynihan, D.P., *Academic Questions*, Winter 96-7, p.32.

11. Herman, Arthur, *Joseph McCarthy*, 2000.

12. Braley, Russ, *Bad News: Of the NY Times*, 1984, Chapter II.

13. Ibid., p. 57.

14. Powell, S.S., *Covert Cadre*, "Inside IPS" with Introduction by David Horowitz, 1987, p. 28.

15. Ibid.

16. Braley, Op. cit.

17. Ibid., p. 202-3.

18. Higgins, Marguerite, *Our Vietnam Nightmare*, 1965, p. 6.

19. Ibid., p. 11.

20. Hammer, Ellen J., *A Death in November*, 1987, p. 275.

21. Braley, op. cit., p. 218.

22. *Newsweek*, 3,19,1990, p. 77.

23. Higgins, op. cit., p. 187.

24. Hammer, op. cit., p. 300,301.

25. Braley, op. cit., p. 381 and 641.

26. *Harper's*, October, 1983, "Life of Kennedy's Death" by Christopher Lasch.

27. NY *Times*, 11,25,1963.

28. *Wall Street Journal*, "Bui Tin Interview", 8,3,1995.

29. Karnow, S. *Vietnam History*, 1983, p. 590.

30. Murphy, D.D., *Conservative Review*, 3-4, 1993; also James Michener's *Kent State*.

31. Ibid.

32. Safire, Wm., *Before The Fall*, 1975, p. 364.

33. Colodny, L. and Gettlin, R., *Silent Coup*, 1991, Forward, by Roger Morris (Nixon aide who left in a huff over Cambodia), p. xxii.

34. Ibid., p. xxiii.

35. Adler, Renata, *Atlantic Monthly*, "Searching for the Nixon Scandal", Dec. 1976, p. 76.

36. Higgins, op. cit., p. 33.

37. Colodny and Gettlin, op, cit., p. xxii and xxiii.

38. Parloff, R., *The American Lawyer*, 6,1992.

39. Brownfield, A.C., *Human Events*, 6,20,92, p. 9.

40. Paula Zahn, CBS, "Morning Show", and *Wall Street Journal*, Editorial, 5,8,92.

41. Ibid.

CHAPTER IX   HATRED AND TRUTH

1. Gelernter, David, *Commentary*, 3,97, p. 37.

2. Breindel, E., 3,30,98, p. 39, A Review of Patricia Bosworth's *Family*.

3. Johnson, P., *Modern Times*, p. 114-122, 282.

4. *Wall Street Journal*, 12,16,98 and 12,21,98.

5. Review of H. Stein's book by R. Radosh, *Commentary*, 9,00, p. 83.

6. Neuhaus, R.J., *The Naked Public Square*, 1984, p.56.

7. *The New American*, 11,8,99, p. 44.

8. Buchanan, J.M., The *Independent Review*, vol. V., No. 1, Summer 2000, p. 111.

9. Houston, Jan Van, *Wall Street Journal*.

10. *J. Social, Political and Economic Studies*, Vol. 18, No. 1. Spring 1993, D.D. Murphy, p. 93, also *National Review*, 11,15,93.

11. Rhenquist, Wm. H., *American Heritage*, 10,1998, p.77.

12. *The American Spectator*, 8,95, p. 28 and 11,95, p. 80.

13. Fumento, M., *Commentary*, 10,96, p. 57.

14. Bovard, J. *Wall Street Journal*, 1,10,95.

15. *The American Spectator*, 12,97, p. 59; and *The New American*, 9,11,00,p.44.

16. *The American Spectator*, 12,97, p. 31.

17. Kopel, David, *The American Enterprise*, 7-8, 95, p. 73.

18. Bovard, op cit.

19. Kopel, David, *The American Enterprise*, 7-8,95, p. 72.

20. Bovard, James, *The American Enterprise*, 12,97, p. 59.

21. *Middle Am. News*, 2,96, p. 14.

22. Kelley, Dean, *First Things*, 5,95, p. 22.

23. Grigg, W.N., *The New American*, 4,13,98, p. 28.

24. Kelley, op. cit., p. 27.

25. Bovard, J., *The New Republic*, 5,15,95, p. 18.

26. Kelley, op. cit., p.25.

27. Bovard, op. cit., p. 18.

28. Kelley, op. cit., p. 25.

29. Kelley, op. cit., p. 31,34.

30. Bovard, op. cit., p.18.

31. Kelley, op. cit., p. 33.

32. Grigg, op. cit., p. 29.

33. Grigg, op. cit., p. 30.

34. *Newsweek*, 7,24,00.

35. Kaplan, R., *Atlantic Monthly*, 2,94.

36. Peretz, Martin, *The New Republic*, 6,18,01.

37. Jones, E. Michael, *Culture Wars*, 12,97, p.45. See also Ibid. p 22-33.

38. Stern, J.P., *Encounter*, 7,88, p.27.

39. James E. Michael, *Culture Wars*, 9,97,p.32.

40. *The New Republic*, 7,28,86, p.4.

41. *New York Times*, 11,23,97. Also *The New American*, 1,5,98, p. 6.

42. Reisman, Dr. Judith, *The New American* 1,4,99, p.36 and 5,24,99 p.29. See also her books, *Kinsey*, 1980, and 1998.

43. Ibid. See also Jones E. Michael, *Culture Wars*, 9,97, p. 36 and 38.

44. Ibid. 4,00, p. 24-31.

45. *Ibid.* 3,01, p.17.

NOTE ON RACISM

1. Saint Exupéry, Antoine de, *Wind, Sand and Stars*, 1940, p. 156,7.

2. *National Review*, 5,14,90, p. 36.

3. Morison, S.E., *Oxford History of American People*, 1965, p. 520.

4. Lincoln, A., Peoria Speech, 10,16,1854: also First Debate, 8,21,1858. Or see *Lincoln*, Vol. I, Library of

America, p. 326.

5. IBID., p. 316.

6. Richburg, K.B., *Out of America*, rev. in *Am. Enterprise*, 7,97, and *Accuracy in Media*, 7,97.

7. Paton, Alan, *Cry, The Beloved Country*, 1948, p. 118.

8. Flack, H.E., *The Adoption of the Fourteenth Amendment*, 1908, p. 146. Also Adams, J.T., *The March of Democracy*, Vol. II, Chapt. III, p. 70.

9. Schwartz, J., *Public Interest*, Spring, 1991, "The Moral Equivalent", p. 31.

10. See: *Wall Street Journal*, Editorial, 6,18,87; *Nat. Review*, 2,22,85, p. 25, *Detroit News*, Cathy Young, Oct. 87.

11. Snyder, J., *Public Interest*, "A Nation of Cowards", (1993).

12. *Conservative Chronicles*, 12,25,96, p. 18.

13. *Newsweek*, 6,10,91, p. 45.

14. *The New Republic*, 12, 21,92, p. 30.

15. Neuhaus, R.J., *The Naked Public Square*, p. 56.

16. *The New American*, 11,8,99, p. 44.

17. *Insight*, 6,5,00, p. 45; and 7,31,00. See also "Thought Reform 101" at www.reason.com or www.thefire.org of A.C.Kors, p. 167.

17A. *Middle American News*, 4,02,p.5. Black attacker Jerell Thomas who killed Kime and attacked two other whites, unlike the killers of James Byrd, was given 15 years in prison; will be out in 5 years.

18. Eisenberg, D., *The New American*, 6,19,00, p. 13.

19. Spiro, G., *Marxism and the Bolshevik State*, p. 781, and E. Silberner, *Historia Judaica*, article on "French Socialism", pp. 6, 7, 4, 1954.

20. Marx-Engels, *Briefwechsel*, July 30, 1862.

21. Marx, K., *Selected Essays*, ed. 1926, p. 88.

22. IBID., p. 90.

23. Liebknecht, Wilhelm, *Karl Marx - Biographical*, 1901, p. 19.

24. Marx, K., *Manifesto*, Translated by Samuel Moore, 1888, p. 11.

25. Egbert and Persons, editors, *Socialism in American Life*, Vol. I, 1952, article by E. H. Harbison.

26. Sweezy, P.M., *Science and Society*, Winter 1948, p. 65.

27. Silberner, op. *Scripta Hierosolymitana*, Jerusalem, 1956, "Anti-Semetic Tradition in Modern Socialism", p. 378, 379.

28. Silberner, E., *Historia Judaica*, April 1954, p. 13.

29. Shils, E.A., Introduction to Sorel's *Reflections*, American Edition.

30. Spiro, op. cit., 1956, p. 790.

31. Marx, K., *Selected Essays*, "Hegelian Philosophy of the Right", p. 33.

32. Hitler, A., *Mein Kampf*, 1940, p. 82.

33. Watson, Geo., *Politics and Literature*, 1977.

34. *Neue Rheinische Zeitung*, Jan. 1849; also see Geo. Watson, *Encounter*, 5,90, p. 79.

35. Watson, Geo., *Idea of Liberalism*.

36. Greider, Wm., *The New Republic*, 5,25,92, p. 39.

37. *Chronicles*, 6,00, p. 29.

38. MacDonald, Kevin, *Culture of Critique*, 6,00, p. 27, and *American Renaissance*, 3,99, p. 6.

39. Rubenstein, R, L., *Commentary*, 8,96, p. 80.

40. Silberner, E., *Scripta Hierosolymitana*, p. 382.

41. Novak, M., *Commentary*, 7-8, 99, p.20. Also *Culture Wars*, 111,97, p. 26.

42. Marx, Karl, *Selected Essays*, "On the Jewish Question", also *Deutsch Franzsiche Jahrbucher*, Feb. 1844.

"ON THE JEWISH QUESTION"

1. Madigan, Kevin, *Commentary*, 10,01 p. 44.

2. Novak, Michael, *Commentary*, 1,02, p. 12.

3. Mayer, Arno, *Why Did The Heavens Not Darken*, 1988; reviewed in *Newsweek*, 5,15,89, p. 64.

4. Shtromas, Aleksandras, *The World And I*, 2,1992, p. 559.

5. Rubenstein, Richard, *Commentary*, 8,96, p. 81.

6. Ravitch, Norman, *Commentary*, 4,98, p. 12.

7. Prager, Dennis, *Commentary*, 8,96, p. 78.

8. Levy, R.S., *Commentary*, 4,98, p. 12.

9. Jones, E.M., *Culture Wars*, 5,00, p.29.

10. Gessman, Dr. A.M., *Issues*, Winter 69.

11. Berkovitz, Rabbi E., *Judaism*, Winter 66.

12. Cohen, Israel, *Congressional Record*, 6,7, 1957.

13. Rubenstein, R.L., *After Auschwitz*; *The New Republic*, 12,3,90, p.

14. Novak, David, *This World*, Winter 89.

15. Wieseltier, Leon, *The New Republic*, *12,3,90, p. 42.*

16. *Commentary*, 1,02, p. 14.

17. Madigan, Kevin, *Commentary*, 10,01, p. 44.

18. Novak, Michael, *Commentary*, 1,02, p. 12.

19. Schwartz, Joel, *Public Interest*, No. 103, Spring 1991, p. 27-29.

20. Stern, J.P., *Encounter*, 207 7,88, p.27.

21. Neuhaus, R.J., *The Naked Public Square*, 1984, p.145,161.

22. Reifer, Rabbi Dr. Manfred, *Czernowitz Allgemeine Zeitung*, 9,2, 1933.

23. Johnson, Paul, *Modern Times*, 1983, p. 113-121.

CHAPTER X ON GUIDANCE

1. Durkheim, Emile, *Le Suicide*, 1897, p. 8. Translation.

2. Mannheim, Karl, *Man and Society*, 1940, p.40-53.

INDEX

Abolitionists - 74, 114
Acheson, Dean - 89
Adams, John - 43
Adams, J.T. - 74
Adler, Renata - 108
Aeschylus - 40
America First – 47, 52, 79, 81, 83, 87
American Medical Association - 2, 14
Amistad - 137
Anders, Polish General - 59
Anti Defamation League (ADL) – 83, 86, 87, 120, 144, 148, 154, 157
Arendt, H. – 63, 155
Aristotle – 37, 89
Arnold, M., - 42
Aryan – 25, 26-29, 147, 148, 161
Auden, W.H. - 71
Augustine - 37

Bacchae, (Euripides) - 103, 130
Baldwin, Alec - 114
Barnet, Richard – 94, 97, 99
Baudrillard, Jean - 26
Beard, C.A. - 51, 138
Beichman, Arnold - 113
Benda, Julien - 116
Berkovitz, Rabbi - 156, 159
bigot - 64
Bissell, Col. - 57
black church burnings hoax - 86
Bloom, Allen - 7, 17
Boas, F. - 5, 151
Bradlee, Ben - 106
Bratton, Col. - 54, 55, 56
Bridges, H. - 113
British Foreign Office – 49, 152

Brooks, Dr. Amanda Lee - 137
Browder, Earl - 81
Buchanan, James - 115
Budenz, Louis - 89
Bui Tin - 104
Bullard, Sara - 147
Bullitt, Wm. C. - 49, 60
Burchett, Wilfred - 96
Bureau of Alcohol, Tobacco, and Firearms, (BATF) - 119, 123,
Butler, Nicholas Murray - 66
Byrd, James - 145

Calvinists - 63
Cambodia – 95, 97, 104, 105
Carlson, John Ray - 87
Carr brothers - 146
Castro, F. - 93, 95
Ceaser, J.M. - 26
Chall, Dr. Jeanne - 68, 69
Chambers, W. - 6, 20, 48
change - 144
Childe, V. Gordon - 28
Chomsky, Noam - 114, 155
Christian - 3, 20, 23, 40, 44, 63, 116, 152-156, 158, 163, 16
Chubb and Moe - 72
church burnings - 119
Church, Frank – 97, 105
Church Committee - 108
Churchill, W. – 47, 48, 50, 53, 55, 62, 82
Cinqué - 137
civilization – 20, 24, 136
Clinton, Hillary – 61 91, 119
Clinton, Wm. - 9, 61, 91, 114, 119, 124
cognitive program - 30
Cohen, I. - 156
Cohen, M. - 3, 5, 73, 93
Cohen, Felix - 73
Coleman Report – 71, 72
Collins, Marva - 68
Communism – 8, 62, 65, 82, 89, 90, 103, 116, 117

computers (ed) - 72
consciousness - 31, 36
conspiracy - 13, 66, 81, 102
Constable - 38
Constitution - 13, 48, 73, 77, 157, 158
Crocker, G. - 51
Cronkite, W. - 102
Cuba - 93
culture – 17, 23, 30, 33, 34, 38, 40
Currie, Lauchlin – 81, 94

Damerell, Reginald - 71
Davidians – 122-126
Davies, Amb. J.E. - 50
Dawidowicz, L. - 7
Dean, John - 102, 108
Deane, Gen. J.R. - 60
Dees, M. - (Southern Poverty Law Center) - 144, 148
de Klerk, F.W. - 128
democracy - 43
Derounian, Avedes, alias John Ray Carlson - 87
Dewey, John - 5, 66, 73, 93
Diem (Ngo Dinh Diem) – 66, 67, 95, 98, 99, 100, 101, 103
Dies, Martin, Reo. - 80
Dingle, John - 122
DNA - 35
Doar, John - 108
Dohrn Bernadine - 105
Donaldson, Sam - 110
Douglas, W.O. - 99
Dresden - 59
Dreyfus Affair - 149
Drumond, Edouard - 150
Dryden, John - 164
Duby, Deanne - 115, 144
Duetschke, Rudi - 116
Durkheim, Emile - 37, 165

Eagleton, Terry - 165
Economists - 4

education - 24, 65-73
Eibl-Eibesfeldt - 33
Elliot, Jane - 144
Ellsberg, Daniel - 91
Enlightenment - 4, 24, 41, 112, 136, 152, 157

Fauré, G.U. - 21, 38
Flack, Horace - 75
Flesch, Dr. Rudolf - 67
Fontenelle, Bernard de - 168
Fourteenth Amendment (14th)– 75, 76, 77, 138, 148, 157
Foxman, Abe - 148
Frankfurt School - 103, 130, 151
Fraser, Doug - 80
Freud - 130
Friedan, (nee Goldstein) Betty - 130, 131
Friedman, W.F. - 50, 57
Fuller, Gen. J.F.C. - 47, 48

Galbraith, John Kenneth - 98
Gallaudet, T.H. - 67
Garrison, Wm. L. (The Liberator) - 75
Gerow, Gen. - 54, 57
Goetz, Bernard - 139, 140
Goldberg, Michelle - 114
government - 12, 13
Gramsci - 5, 117
Great Sedition Trial - 83
Greeks – 3, 4, 19, 20, 39, 115, 116, 167, 168
Grew, Amb. Joseph – 53, 82
Gumbel, B. – 117, 142

Halberstam, David - 100
Hall, G. Stanley - 65
Hand, Judge Learned - 78
Harriman, Averill – 99, 100
hate crimes - 144-148
hatred - 22, 102, 107, 112, 113, 125, 126, 144, 145
Hegel, Georg Wilhelm - 42, 153, 166
Hellman, Lillian - 113

Higgins, Marguerite - 109
Hilsman, Roger - 100
Hiss, Alger – 47, 90, 94, 96
Hitler, Adolf – 150, 151
Hobbes, Thomas - 38, 99
Ho Chi Minh - 100, 104
Hochhuth, Rolf - 154, 157
Hollywood Ten (Communists) - 65
"Holocaust" – 152, 152, 154, 156, 157, 159
Hooker, Richard - 25
Hopkins, Harry - 48, 56, 60, 61, 81, 94
Hoover, Herbert - 47
Hull, Cordell - 53, 55, 57, 82
Human Rights Watch - 29
Huxley, T.H. - 42, 130

Ice-T - 142
ideas - 37
immigration – 127-129, 158
Impeachment of Nixon - 106-109
Institute for Policy Studies (IPS) - 94-97

Jackson, Jesse - 142
Japanese – 46, 47, 48, 52, 53, 54, 118
Japanese Purple Code - 50
Japanese spies - 55, 118
Jaures, Jean - 150
Jews – 84, 114, 151, 158, 160
Johnson, L.B. – 91, 101, 103, 104
Johnson, Paul - 59, 113, 153, 159
Johnson Sidney - 105
Johnson, Samuel - 29, 22, 164

Kant, Immanuel - 37
Kennan, G.F. - 58
Kennedy, J.F. – 87, 91, 94, 100, 101, 102, 103, 147
Kennedy, Robert – 99, 101
Kent State - 105
Kime, Cristopher - 145
Kimmel, Adm., H.E. - 55

King, Adm. E.J. - 57
King, M.L. - 161
King, Rodney - 61, 109, 110, 117
Kinsey, Alfred - 130-133
Klein, Henry - 84
Konoye, Prince - 52, 53, 82
Kramer, Capt. A.D. - 55

language - 43
Lassalle, F. - 149, 153, 159
Leahy, Adm. W.D. - 47, 59
Leakey, R. - 38
Lee, Spike - 142, 143
Lend-Lease - 60
Lenin - 9, 39, 112, 41, 49, 161
Letelier, Orlando - 97
Liberal Project and Papers - 94, 154, 155
Lincoln, A. - 74, 75
Lindberg, C. - 81, 84
Lippmann, W. - 5, 45, 48, 64, 77, 95, 113, 117, 138
Lodge, H.C. - 99-101
Lorenz, K. - 17, 32, 33
Luce, Clare Boothe - 82
Lyons, Eugene - 8, 50

MacArthur, Gen. Douglas - 57, 59
Machiavelli, Niccolo - 4, 25, 112, 130, 153
Madison James - 73
"Magic" – 50, 53, 55, 82, 118
Mann, Horace - 63, 65
Mannheim, Karl - 165
Marshall, Gen. G. – 53, 56, 57, 58, 89
Marx, Karl – 39, 44, 112, 116
Matthews, Herb – 93, 95, 100
McCarthy, Sen. Joseph – 64, 65, 88, 89, 90
McCollum, Capt. A.N. - 56
Mead, Margaret - 130, 169
Mill, J.S. - 23, 30, 167
Miller, Arthur – 109, 110
Morgenthau Plan - 98

Morison, S.E. - 64, 82
Motion Picture Academy - 113
Moynihan, Sen. Daniel P. - 61, 91
Murrow, E. R. - 89, 100

NAACP - 142, 149
Navasky, Victor - 113
Nazis - 49, 79, 148
NEA (Nat. Ed. Assn.) – 63, 66, 68, 71, 127, 137
Newman, John Cardinal - 5
New York Times - 8, 87, 89, 95, 97, 102, 105, 110, 131, 133, 139, 148, 153
Newsweek – 110
Nietzsche, F.H. - 17, 22, 24, 112, 130
Nimitz, Adm. C.W. - 59
Nixon, Richard – 104-111
Nolting, Amb. Fredrick - 100
Novak, Michael – 152, 155
Novak, David - 156
Nuremberg Trials - 87

Oakeshott, Michael - 24
Orton, Dr. S. T. - 67, 68
Oswald, Lee Harvey - 102
Outcome Based Education (OBE) - 72

Paleolithic artists – 21, 38
parental tenderness – 34
Parloff, Roger - 110
Paton, Alan S. - 130
Pearl Harbor (reports) - 46, 51, 57
Pentagon Papers – 91, 95, 96, 101
Pfeffer, Leo - 155
phonics - 67-69
"pilot" message - 55
Plato - 39
politics - 13
Pope Pius XII – 49, 154, 157
Powers, Richard Gid - 87
Powers, Richard H. - 73

Prager, D. - 155
provocateurs - 87, 147
Puritans - 63, 64, 115
purpose - 15, 16

Quang (Tri Quang) - 100
Quayle, D. - 114
Quigleys - 148
Quigley, C. - 9

Rabinowitz, Dorothy - 79
racism – 136-152
Raskin, Marcus - 94
Ravitch, Diana - 69
Reagan, Ronald - 115
reason - 31, 32, 34
Reconstruction – 74-76
Reich, Wilhelm - 130, 131, 154, 166
Reifer, Rabbi Dr. Manfred - 159
Reisman, Judith - 133
religion - 10, 37, 163, 166-170, 165
Reno, J. - 121
Richardson, Adm. J. - 51
Richburg, Keith - 137
Riis, Jacob - 139, 157
Rocker, John - 142
Rogge, O. John – 83, 85, 88
Roosevelt, Franklin - 45-60, 65, 77-83, 109, 113, 117, 118
Roosevelt, Eleanor - 60, 81
Roosevelt, Elliott - 46, 60
Rubenstein, J. - 115
Rubenstein, R.L. - 151, 152, 155, 156, 159
Ruby Ridge - 119

Sade, Comte de - 31
Sadtler, Col. O.K. – 54, 56
Safford, Commdr. L.F. - 57
Safire, Wm. - 110
Saint Exupéry, Antoine de - 136
sanctuaries - 104, 105

Sandel, M.J - 14
Schiller, von, J.C.F. - 38
Schlesinger, A.M. Jr. - 6, 46, 51, 57, 87, 89
schools - 63-75
Schrecker, Ellen - 65, 88
Schulz, Comdr. L. R. - 55
Schumpeter, J.A. - 10
Schweitzer, Albert - 5, 22
Seattle Mardi Gras (2001) - 145
Sedition Trial - 83-88
SDS (Students for a Democratic Society) - 105
sex education - 72, 133
sex revolution - 72-133
Shaw, G.B. - 150
Shishmaroff, de, Paquita - 85
Shtromas, A. - 155
Short, Gen. W.C. - 56
Sihanouk, Premier - 104
Simon, John - 70
Slaughterhouse Cases - 76
Sleeper, J. - 138
Smith, Col. W. B. - 55, 56
Snow, C. P. - 41
Social Contract - 18
society - 17-20, 34, 37
Solomon - 39, 163
Sowell, Tom - 110, 112, 139
Stalin, J. – 47, 59, 65, 83, 150
Stalin - Hitler Pact – 52, 89, 87
Stark, Adm. H.R. - 57
Stein, Harry - 114
Stern, Van Doren - 38
Stevens, Thad - 75, 138
Stimson, H.L. - 98
Stokes, Dillard - 83
Stone, Oliver - 143, 147, 151
syntactic language - 33

Tawney, R.H. - i
Tet-1968, 104

Three Rs - 70
Tocqueville, Alex de - 4, 12, 13, 41
totalitarianism - 3, 4, 19, 21
Tri Quang – 100
Trilling, Lionel - 38
Trotskyite "manifesto" - 50
Truman, Harry S. - 65, 89, 91, 147
truth - 31
Tyack, David - 66

Van Buren, Abigail - 117
"Vagina Monologues" - 134
"Verona" - 61, 65, 81, 92
Vietnam - 95-105
Voltaire - 112, 152

Waco - 9, 62, 121-126
Wagschal, Peter - 69
"War Warning" - 54
Ward, Barbara – 5
Warren, Earl - 102, 118
Warren Commission - 102
Washington Post – 83, 86, 97, 106, 121, 137
Watergate – 91, 107
Weaver, Randy - 121, 122
Weber, Max - 4, 24
Wedemeyer, Gen. A.C. - 48, 152
Weinstein, Allen - 90
Wieseltier, Leon - 157
Weiss, Cora - 96, 97
Weiss, Philip - 158
Wells, H.G. - 150
Wheeler, Sen. B.K. – 81, 84
Wilson, Edmund - 113
"winds" message - 53, 55
witch hunting - 64, 65
Wolfe, Alan - 69
Wolfe, Tom - 142

Yahoos - 112, 115, 144

Yalta - 51, 59, 109

Zahn, Paula - 110